Also Available from EYE ON EDU...

Assessing Middle and High School Social Studies and English: Differentiating Formative Assessment
Sheryn Spencer Waterman

Differentiating Assessment in Middle and High School English and Social Studies
Sheryn Spencer Waterman

Handbook on Differentiated Instruction for Middle & High Schools
Sheryn Spencer Northey

Critical Thinking and Formative Assessments: Increasing the Rigor in Your Classroom
Betsy Moore and Todd Stanley

Differentiated Assessment for Middle & High School Classrooms
Deborah Blaz

Teacher-Made Assessments: Connecting Curriculum, Instruction, and Student Learning
Christopher R. Gareis and Leslie W. Grant

Formative Assessment for English Language Arts: A Guide for Middle and High School Teachers
Amy Benjamin

Teaching Grammar: What Really Works
Amy Benjamin and Joan Berger

Empowering Students to Write and Re-write: Strategies for Middle and High School Teachers
Warren E. Combs

Active Literacy Across the Curriculum: Strategies for Reading, Writing, Speaking, and Listening
Heidi Hayes Jacobs

Formative Assessment: Responding to Your Students
Harry Grover Tuttle

Successful Student Writing Through Formative Assessment
Harry G. Tuttle

Meet the Authors

Arthur K. Ellis is Professor of Education and Director of the Center for Global Curriculum Studies at Seattle Pacific University. Before that, he was Professor of Education at the University of Minnesota. Dr. Ellis taught elementary and middle school in Oregon and Washington before completing his doctorate at the University of Oregon. He also holds honorary doctorates from the University of the Russian Academy of Education and is a Corresponding Professor at three universities in Russia. He also works closely with the College of Education and Department of Philosophy at Zhejiang University in China. Several of his books have been published in Russian, Chinese, and Korean versions. Among his more recent publications is a study of Service Learning published by the Japanese Research Institute of Higher Education.

Laurynn Evans, an experienced teacher and administrator, has worked with students and staff for more than fifteen years in two different states in a variety of roles. She has been a classroom teacher, a teacher on special assignment focused on staff development, a high school assistant principal, and a building principal. Her work has led her to teach in a variety of settings ranging from middle school to the collegiate level, as well as afforded her the opportunity to work with students from diverse backgrounds, ranging from high-poverty and high-needs demographics to upper-level graduate students. She recently completed her doctorate in education at Seattle Pacific University and is currently a junior high school principal in the Seattle area.

Acknowledgments

The origins of this book can be traced back to a grant from the Albertson Foundation and the work that was done with teachers for that group in the area of formative assessment of student learning. That experience gave us splendid opportunities to field test the assessment strategies found in the pages that follow.

Beyond that we are indebted to a number of people who have continued to test these strategies in both field work and in controlled research studies. We are especially grateful to Richard Scheuerman, John Bond, Kathy Shoop, and David Denton for the efforts they made to test and refine these ideas with students in school settings.

Teaching, Learning, & Assessment Together

Reflective Assessments for Middle & High School English & Social Studies

Arthur K. Ellis & Laurynn Evans

EYE ON EDUCATION
6 DEPOT WAY WEST, SUITE 106
LARCHMONT, NY 10538
(914) 833–0551
(914) 833–0761 fax
www.eyeoneducation.com

A sincere effort has been made to supply the identity of those who have created specific strategies. Any omissions have been unintentional.

Library of Congress Cataloging-in-Publication Data

Ellis, Arthur K.

   Teaching, learning & assessment together : reflective assessments for middle & high school English & social studies / Arthur K. Ellis, Laurynn Evans.

      p. cm.

   ISBN 978-1-59667-158-4

   1. English language—Study and teaching (Middle school) 2. English language—Study and teaching (Secondary) 3. Social sciences—Study and teaching (Middle school) 4. Social sciences—Study and teaching (Secondary) 5. Effective teaching. I. Evans, Laurynn. II. Title. III. Title: Teaching, learning, and assessment together.

   LB1631.E53 2010

   428.0071'2—dc22

                                                        2010007776

10 9 8 7 6 5 4 3 2 1

Contents

Preface

Follow effective action with quiet reflection. From the quiet reflection will come even more effective action.

— Peter F. Drucker (1990)

The great Renaissance scholar Erasmus wrote that "reflection is a flower of the mind." This beautiful metaphor serves as a reminder that experience and activity, although necessary elements of education, are not sufficient. Only when we thoughtfully reflect do the seeds of experience and activity reach full flower. The economist Peter Drucker (1990), quoted above, insightfully points out that action improves with reflection, which in turn leads to more effective action. This comment on the reciprocal nature of action and reflection is crucial to any academic improvements we wish to make. Active learning has the potential to engage students in a process John Dewey (1938, 1997) called "knowledge as action."

The Greek philosopher Aristotle also called to our attention the principle that "for the things we have to learn before we can do them, we learn by doing them" (Adler, 1952, p. 348). Aristotle informs of the necessity of *experience and activity* in learning. To this, Confucius, another ancient sage, adds that "experience without reflection is labor lost" (*The Analects*, book ii, xv). When purposeful activity is examined reflectively by students and teachers, then a value-added component emerges. Reflective practice allows us to make sense of activity, to question its benefits, to seek ways to improve, and to take responsibility for learning. This is the "flower of the mind." This is the means by which achievement is increased.

This book is designed to help you realize two goals: (1) raising academic achievement and (2) improving the social/moral fabric of school life. To accomplish these two goals, we will explore and develop the relationships among three important but seldom connected endeavors: teaching, learning, and assessment.

Research studies by Tindal and Nolet (1996) and Pellegrino (2006) suggest that teaching, learning, and assessment are often misaligned and that more needs to be done to unite these important dimensions of education. Nevertheless, if the message of this book is successful, you will come to think of the three as inseparable. The idea is that these three elements of school life need to be considered as seamless, they must not be separated. To the extent that you act on this idea, you will be well on the way toward the development of a reflective classroom.

Three Inseparables

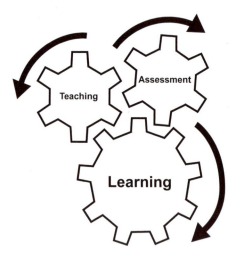

What would such a classroom be like? How would such a classroom be different from an ordinary classroom? Here is a little test for you to take as you begin reading this book.

Circle your response (yes, no, or unsure) to the following statements:

1. yes no unsure Student achievement is clearly emphasized in my classroom.

2. yes no unsure Students need to be consistently aware of their academic progress.

3. yes no unsure Students need to talk with each other about what they are learning.

4. yes no unsure Often, too little time is given to students to reflect on their learning.

5. yes no unsure Assessment should be integrated with teaching and learning.

6. yes no unsure Learning will improve if student are given opportunities to reflect.

7. yes no unsure The curriculum "coverage" mentality defeats in-depth learning.

8. yes no unsure Without reflection, "in one ear and out the other" happens.

9. yes no unsure Social/moral growth represents a key educational goal.

Whatever your response to these statements, we urge you to talk about your sense of them with another fellow professional. Indeed, if you are participating in a professional learning community, we urge you to read this book with a colleague. At the conclusion of each chapter, there are discussion questions to guide personal as well as collegial growth. At any rate, if you do discuss your "test" results, you will be participating in reflective thinking and reflective assessment.

What This Book Is About

This is a book filled with old ideas. For centuries the wisest people from cultures around the world have asked us to practice reflection. In recent times, empirical research has shown such thinking to be correct. The irony is that so few teachers practice reflective thinking with their students. The good news is that the strategies are easy to use, do not take much class time, and cost nothing. They work with younger learners as well as older learners, and they can be used across a wide range of subject matter areas, from beginning reading to physical education, to advanced mathematics. And they *will* work.

This book will help you align teaching, learning, and assessment through reflective practice. Each chapter begins with a *reflective teaching strategy*. This is followed with *related theory and professional learning community discussion questions*. There are *research insights* relating to the topic at hand. *Guiding icons* will help you coordinate and implement the strategies with your students.

Reflective Practice

Study without reflection is a waste of time.
— Confucius

This is a book about practical ways to create a classroom environment where teaching, learning, and assessment come together to form a seamless whole. The vehicle for making this happen is reflective practice. Reflective practice means not just doing things, covering the curriculum, carrying out assignments, and preparing for tests, but taking time to dig beneath the surface to unearth questions of purpose, meaning, value, and belonging. Even in "better" classroom situations, reflective practice is the all-too-often-missing ingredient, the factor that, if it *were* present, makes the difference between school as "that place you have to go to" and school as "that place you want to go to." Reflective practice is about caring, collaboration, integration, affiliation, and truth in teaching and learning.

When people are introduced to the strategies found in this text, they are initially of different opinions about whether the activities are in fact teaching, learning, or assessment strategies. Our answer is invariably this: They are all three at once. They will change the way you and your students teach, the way you and your students learn, and the way you and your students assess hope, growth, and opportunity. They are designed to be small-scale activities, with a focus on the classroom. The strategies work best in situations where *strategic teaching, active learning, and reflective assessment are one.*

We mentioned that the strategies are practical. Indeed they are, and in that spirit we make this promise: If you use them faithfully and consistently two things will happen. First, you and your students will notice achievement gains. Standardized test scores will reflect these gains, but the achievement gains you and your class will experience will be far greater than can be shown by such narrow measures of growth. Second, you and your students will come to know that the social/moral fabric of your school life has improved greatly. Standardized tests seldom take social and moral growth into account. This is a reminder that such tests have a purpose, albeit a rather limited one.

We also stated earlier that this is a practical book with practical applications. This is because teaching is practical. Teaching is situated, that is, it happens at a particular time in a particular place with real people. Only those who have never been in the classroom would offer a different opinion. But excellent practice inevitably can be traced to theory. There are powerful ideas behind it. Our experience with teachers and administrators, especially those who strive for excellence, is that they do care about where ideas come from. This is precisely why this book contains a series of very brief essays detailing the theoretical considerations that underlie the activities. Each essay was originally considerably longer. We have distilled them to their essence. Those who wish to probe more deeply are invited to do so by investigating the references found at the end of this book.

Then there are the strategies themselves. Each is designed to help you and your students step back from whatever it is that you are doing and to reflect on the experience. These are *activities,* that is, they are things you do. Some of them call for writing, others for discussion, others for drawing, investigating, recording, record keeping, and other forms of reflection. Each activity can be thought of as a lesson template. In other words, the activities use class time and homework in the same sense that other activities do. The strategies represent an academic quest as well as a social/moral quest. Academic, social, and moral growth represent the goal structure of the book.

The (Hoped for) Outcomes

Arriving at one goal is the starting point to another.
— John Dewey

If this book succeeds in its intended purpose, you and your students will realize two important outcomes. First, you will see improved achievement. This will happen as students learn to monitor their own progress, become self-regulated learners, and improve their sense of awareness of what and why they are learning. Second, your classroom will become a place with a deepened social/moral fabric. This will happen as students think and talk together about what they are learning, share their knowledge and skills with each other, and realize how enjoyable group life in a classroom can be.

Learning Community Discussion Starters

1. How are academic achievement and the social/moral fabric of a classroom connected?

2. What kinds of teacher behaviors need to be in place in order to develop a reflective classroom?

Guiding Icons Defined

 Cooperation: This example proposes ways to integrate cooperative learning and reflective activities together.

 Dig Deep: Here, you will read about ideas to enrich the strategy for students who are ready for an additional challenge and advanced level of learning.

 Insights from Research: This material describes some characteristic of reflective thinking and its use as an instructional practice.

 Look for: This discussion describes changes you might see in your classroom if reflective thinking and strategies are used over the long-term.

 Mix and Match: As the old saying goes, two is better than one. *Mix and Match* describes ways to combine reflective strategies to produce different results or to give the strategy an interesting twist.

 Simplify: Instructional strategies are only as useful as they are feasible. Here you will find tips on streamlining the strategy with regard to such topics as reducing paperwork and efficient grading.

 Support: Certainly, classrooms are becoming more diverse. *Support* offers useful and simple ideas to assist all types of learners.

Tech Tip: Today, many classrooms are stocked with a variety of instructional equipment. Here you will find tips on integrating the reflective strategy with classroom technology, ranging from document cameras to overhead projectors.

I Learned

The reasonable thing is to learn from those who can teach.

— Sophocles

Purpose

The *I Learned** statement for assessing learning is a quick and efficient way to get a sense of your students' grasp of a lesson or activity. It is beautifully simple, and it achieves two assessment goals at once: (1) each student gives you feedback on what he or she thought was of significance, and (2) the aggregate of the responses informs you to what extent you achieved your teaching goal. Remember that *the purpose of school is not teaching—it is learning.* Teaching is something one does in order to create opportunities for learning.

Procedure

Here is how the process works. At the conclusion of a class period, with five minutes or so left, ask each student to write down on a sheet of paper, "I learned such and such…" in today's activity or lesson. For example, if you have just taught students about the relationship between cause and effect in a historical conflict, an *I Learned* statement by one student might read, "I learned that tension between Germany and France led to World War II." Although such a reflective comment does not answer the "why" or address the *concept* of cause and effect, it does at least get at the "what." The student has shown that he or she knows an example of cause and effect in relation to historical events. If few or no reflective statements indicate *why* (the concept) cause and effect is important, this helps *you* assess the lesson, which is an added purpose of reflective assessment. It could be because you did not explain *why*. Tomorrow you can do just that. Skip ahead in the text to Strategy

---

* A description of the *I Learned* statement is found in S. Simon, L. Howe, and H. Kirschenbaum (1972). *Values Clarification.* New York: Hart Publishing. The strategy is attributed to Jerry Weinstein.

13: *Clear and Unclear Windows* for some early insight into a way you can get at students' deeper understandings.

If you have been studying the water cycle with students, an *I Learned* statement might read, "I learned that water goes through four cycles: evaporation, condensation, precipitation, and collection." In a unit where students are engaged in cooperative leaning, an *I Learned* statement could read, "I learned that working together means we have to find out what others think." Such simple statements are a reasonable place to begin. As students practice writing statements, particularly in the case of older students, their reflections will begin to take on greater depth, but all this comes with time.

These examples come from students who show some basic understanding of significant skills and/or ideas. Of course, not everyone will grasp the main idea, but the point is that even if this is so you are better off knowing that. It doesn't pay to assume that everyone learned something just because you or I taught it. And when some students do show a grasp of what was taught and others do not, this becomes a perfect moment for peer teaching.

The first time you try *I Learned* statements with your class, don't be surprised if half the papers turned in are blank. This is nothing to be alarmed about. In most cases, students are not asked what they just learned, so they don't tend to think in those terms. In other words, students are not typically asked to reflect. Also, don't be surprised if many of the papers contain "irrelevant" or "inaccurate" *I Learned* statements. Moreover, be sure to share insightful *I Learned* statements by students with the entire class. Some students need examples in order for them to grasp the general idea.

We remember having our students write *I Learned* statements following a presentation by a uniformed naval officer who had spoken to the class. One student's response stays in our thoughts to this day. She wrote, "I learned that they have gold buttons on their coat." It could be argued that this was hardly the main idea of the presentation, which was on the topic of careers, but that is what she said she learned.

One of the joys of *I Learned* assessment comes from statements by students who not only grasp the intent of the lesson but who see in it really good things that you yourself hadn't even considered. This is value-added teaching and learning! In other words, they made connections to some prior knowledge or experience. When students write statements that are insightful and even profound, be sure to read those statements aloud to the class. This will help others to understand the process better.

Sometimes what people need most are good examples to get them started. One of the things you will notice if you use this technique over time is that students get better and better at reflection. Of course, keep in mind that learning is a complex process and that students may learn things that you feel were not intended or even to the point. Who knows what prior knowledge a given individual might bring to an activity and how it might affect their learning? It serves as a good reminder that even though we might think we are teaching exactly the same thing to all thirty students, that is not the case. Each individual must construct his or her *own* knowledge. Invariably people will come up with somewhat different constructions. You need be concerned only if you are convinced that students are not getting the point at all.

It does matter greatly *what* is taught when it comes to assessing *I Learned* statements by students. For example, if you are teaching certain skills that you think are crucial, then you do want to be sure that students are grasping those skills. This is known as *convergent knowledge*; this is especially important in elementary mathematical procedures and in any subject where skills are emphasized. However, if you are teaching complex ideas, it is quite understandable that students might have varied perspectives on those ideas. You have entered the realm of *divergent knowledge*. If you are teaching two-place addition, of course, you will hope to receive *I Learned* statements that are related to the skill. Even in such a case, however, the *insights* that students generate in learning this can vary considerably. And if you are teaching something as complex as social skills to your class, expect a wide range of insights and personal applications from students.

Outcomes

One use of the *I Learned* statement is diagnostic. If you receive a large number of statements that you believe are inaccurate or misleading, you will probably want to try teaching the same material again, perhaps in a different way. If you receive a mix of statements, you may want to form peer-teaching groups in which those who clearly grasp the content or skill are asked to share their knowledge with students who are having trouble with the material.

The aggregate of the *I Learned* responses from a class of students is one of the best indicators of your success in achieving your objective in a lesson. Taken together, a classroom set of statements forms a kind of mosaic reflecting the quality of the experience. You can control what you teach, but you cannot control what is learned. Sometimes they are basically the same thing, and on other days, well, they are worlds apart.

How often should a teacher use *I Learned* statements? The answer is often, but probably not every day. The thing to keep in mind is that you are attempting to raise the level of consciousness of your students. You are asking them to become conscious of what they are learning. In other words, you are asking them to be reflective, to practice *metacognition*, to think about their learning. Like any technique, the *I Learned* statement can be overused. It is best to use it intermittently, perhaps three or four times a week; this way students will have it in the back of their minds that you just might use it on any particular occasion, helping them to be alert to this possibility and to think about what they are learning just in case they are asked. In time it becomes automatic for them to think that way, in which case you will have achieved a very important educational goal.

Differentiating *I Learned* Statements

 Give students only three minutes to write individual *I Learned* statements. Then have them buddy up with one or two peers to craft a group *I Learned* statement with the remaining two to three minutes. This statement could be directed to focus on a particular question that all students shared or a particular "aha" that the group felt was important. Have the group staple all of their individual and group statements together in a packet to help you see the direction of their thought process.

 At the beginning of the next class day, share out example *I Learned* statements with the group by utilizing your document camera. The examples should be anonymous in the event that the reflections share personal insights. Showing student work this way lets students see how their peers were thinking about content, as well as giving them a model to aim toward in their next effort at crafting *I Learned* statements. By showing statements that reference the literature being read or the historical content that was discussed, you push student work toward featuring those elements in future efforts.

 This is a particularly effective strategy for special needs students who suffer from poor organization or recall of learned information. Have students keep and collect their statements in a classroom folder. These statements could then be used by students as part of an in-class review prior to a unit test, quiz, or other culminating activity.

Students who have difficulty writing could be encouraged to draw out their *I Learned* statement or to have a peer scribe their thoughts. Conversely, the cooperative technique outlined above could also be used to assist struggling learners with sharing their thinking and having it be recorded for later review.

 The time given to students can be limited to less than five minutes in order to keep things streamlined and/or simpler. Also, teachers can give specific instructions to target the writing of students towards a particular element of content from the lesson. Remember that for younger students, more guidance on what to write and more concrete directions will help student reflections be more useful to both you and the student.

I Learned statements can be a great way to push the thinking of your higher-achieving students. By requiring students to tie in primary source quotes to substantiate their comments, students connect more deeply with literature or historical documents. By having them use quotes to frame their questions, students are pushed to connect their thinking to the content to which they have been exposed and they gain more confidence in working with primary sources.

 I Learned statements can be combined with a number of other strategies presented in this book. For example, it could be combined with *Think Aloud* (Strategy 2) very easily. At the start of the next period, students could engage in dialogue about their *I Learned* statements and then craft a new and improved statement that encapsulates their best thinking. These statements can also be done in the style of *Search for Meaning* (Strategy 9) with a focus on personal reactions to literature, or could be a "Day in Review" format similar to that of *The Week in Review* (Strategy 3).

 Evans (2009) found that students who wrote and discussed *I Learned* statements daily for the course of a unit of study significantly outperformed their nonreflecting peers on both the unit test (posttest) and on a readministration of that same test five weeks later (retention test). Anecdotal data collected from the students further indicated that the students enjoyed the reflective activity and that they thought it was "very important" in helping them learn and retain new concepts and connections in their learning.

From the Classroom

Crystal Adams is teaching a unit based on the novel "Whirligig" to ninth grade students for three weeks. The novel is being utilized as part of a larger overarching theme for the semester about the Heroic Journey and how it appears in various pieces of literature over time. The novel's storyline requires that students internalize a lot of the main character's feelings and struggles. To help her students grasp the literary elements and themes as well reflect upon the journey undertaken by the main character, Crystal has her students write *I learned* statements at the conclusion of each lesson.

> I learned that the Hero's Journey can be in a lot of different places. I think I now see that it even makes up the storyline in a lot of my favorite movies!

> I learned that everyone has a hidden struggle that we might not see. I also learned that we all feel alone in the world sometimes.

When I read about Brent going to the party and feeling so out of place I knew exactly how he felt. I hate being the new kid too.

I learned that a hero can be almost any character from any story, so long as they have a major challenge to overcome and they follow the steps of the journey we got in class today.

I learned that a lot of my classmates have things that concern them and worry them, and realized that like Brent, a lot of people have problems that might make them sad or angry. When we shared the statements today and we read about one person's struggles at their house, it just hit me that we are all in this together and we should support one another more.

As you can see, the students' *I Learned* statements encompass both academic learning as well as personal insights. Both styles of reflection are certainly acceptable and should be encouraged. Crystal noticed that the caliber of student writing greatly improved by anonymously sharing examples of the statements with the full class at the start of the next class session. She also found that improvement happened by providing timely feedback on the students' writing. More importantly, she reports that students have gained a greater sense of empathy for their peers and classroom morale has vastly improved after repeatedly sharing *I Learned* statements with all students!

What Is Teaching?

There is a time for everything, a season for every activity under heaven.

— Ecclesiastes 3:1

Jean Piaget (1965) defined teaching as the creation of an environment in which students can grow intellectually, socially, and morally. However you define it, a central premise must be acknowledged: *teaching is a means.* Learning, which we will get to in due course, is an *end.*

Two useful images give us a place to begin. One image is that of the *scholar* sharing knowledge, skills, and values with students. The premise is simple: One person knows things that others need to know, and it is the role of that person, the teacher, to somehow get those ideas across to learners. Thus we have an expert working with novices. This is a familiar image. This is the *traditional* description of the teacher. This view of teaching is often criticized by progressives as dated and irrelevant to teaching and learning in today's world. But only when it is carried to excess is this the case. Its greatest strength, however, also contains its potential weakness, and that is the temptation to put subject matter ahead of people. When this happens learning becomes impersonal, and the human connections so desperately needed are lost. It is good to remember the old adage, "people first, procedures second, and tools third."

Another way of thinking about teaching is to consider the teacher as *facilitator*. The image is that of the expert coach, the fellow learner and guide. This is not to say that the teacher should know nothing. Rather, the idea is that of a teacher who wants students to learn for themselves, to explore, discover, construct, and create their own knowledge. Actually, to do this well, a teacher *must* possess knowledge of subject matter.

This teacher is less concerned about traditional notions of separate subjects and more concerned with project learning, with student sharing and team building, and with applications to the world beyond the school. This is a difficult role for some teachers because they want to "give" their knowledge to young learners. The fact is, however, that this is not possible. Each person must finally construct his or her own knowledge of the world. It is helpful to remember Jean Piaget's statement that telling is not teaching. Remember that Piaget described teaching as the organization of environments in which students' intellectual and social/moral growth can emerge. This constitutes a clear shift in the center of gravity from teacher to learner. Finally, the best teachers inspire their students. They lead them to *want* to learn.

Which of these two descriptions of teaching is more effective? Can the two be blended in some meaningful way? The answer to that question is "yes." The high moral road of eclecticism will lead good teachers to see the value in each. This means that a teacher will embody the best of both approaches. The best teachers are both sages *and* guides, and they vary their practice depending on context and situation.

Learning Community Discussion Starters

1. How do you know when to change roles as a teacher from facilitator to sage and back again?

2. What kinds of learning activities are better suited to teacher as facilitator?

3. What is the key to creating a setting conducive to intellectual, social, and moral growth?

4. What does it mean when we refer to the teacher as a model of good learning?

Strategy 2
Think Aloud

The little girl had the making of a poet in her who, being told to be sure of her meaning before she spoke, said, "How can I know what I think 'til I see what I say?"

— Graham Wallas

Purpose

The *Think Aloud* strategy is designed to accomplish three primary goals: (1) creating a self-feedback mechanism, (2) testing one's ideas in public, and (3) making thought processes more intentionally deliberate. The achievement by students of these three goals will go a long way toward creating a reflective perspective in problem solving and other higher-order learning experiences.

Perhaps you've watched a tennis match on television and noticed that some of the players seem to have a habit of talking to themselves. The legendary champion John McEnroe was particularly noted for practicing this behavior on court in front of a stadium full of spectators. Psychologists commenting on McEnroe's self-talk tended to agree that he was doing something very useful. McEnroe's self-talk—often he would berate himself—served as a means of focusing his attention, helping him to concentrate under difficult conditions, and reminding him why he was out there, which was to play his best.

Students trying to solve problems can benefit from this strategy. It really seems to help to talk to oneself in the course of problem solving. It does focus attention on the problem. It does help with concentration. Of course, a classroom might become a trifle noisy if all students are simultaneously talking their way through mathematics problems, but there is no reason why they cannot do this as part of their homework. Self-talk is one form of this strategy. Thinking aloud with a partner is another. When we think aloud, we slow the process down. This is exactly what is needed to clarify our ideas.

Procedure

A simple technique is to require students to talk to each other in pairs as they solve at least one of the problems or assignments given to them as homework. This creates a feedback mechanism that may be the one thing lacking in the student's approach to his or her work. You can set the stage for a pretty good class discussion by asking students how thinking aloud (either through self-talk or with a partner) changes how they think through a problem.

A benefit of the *Think Aloud* strategy derives from expressing our views to someone else. It is often the case that when our thinking goes astray we are the last to know because everything seems fine according to our own interior logic. By keeping our thoughts to ourselves, we lose the benefit of the outside perspective needed to test the validity of our ideas.

But what if my reasoning is obviously (to others) faulty? This is what critics are for, to help us know what we're doing right and possibly wrong. If I tell you how I'm solving a problem, I am given the opportunity to test my logic in a kind of open-air marketplace. And if you are my partner, I get the added benefit of listening to you tell me how you solved the problem.

Outcomes

The benefit is actually double: First, saying out loud how I'm thinking forces me to be clear to myself and others, and second, the process allows you to ask me questions, to challenge my assumptions, and to try to understand me. Thus the talker gains whether the talker was using valid reasoning or not because the process has been "inspected."

Related to these two outcomes is a third: Talking about something you're thinking about forces you to slow down, to be more deliberate. There is good evidence to show that average and below-average learners in particular tend to skip steps in solving problems. In their hurry to accomplish a task, they leave out important procedures that end up making all the difference in the world. The ancient Greek storyteller Aesop reminds us in the tale of "The Tortoise and the Hare" that the race is not necessarily won by the swift, but by the sure.

The student who reads a story quickly does not necessarily understand what he or she has read better than the more deliberate reader. A good artist or poet is seldom judged by how quickly a picture was painted or a verse written. A good craftsman takes his or her time to do a job well. The effect of slowing down learning is greatly undervalued by most teachers. And when you talk about what you're thinking, it slows you down. This is a first step toward quality.

Differentiating *Think Aloud*

 By layering discussion, discourse between and among students deepens and the critical feedback loop is able to thrive. Teachers can have students individually solve problems, with students either talking to themselves or writing out their thoughts (have students put a crease down the center of their paper where they do their work on one side and write out their thinking process on the other). Then have students turn and talk with a neighbor to further their thinking. Finally, pairs of students can meet with other pairs.

 Having students use the written feedback loop where they do their work on one side of a page and then write out their thinking process on the other is a good way to promote students to talk about their thinking process. Teachers can also use verbal prompts with students who might struggle with complex problem solving, especially when that problem solving is happening in more abstract fields like literature and/or history.

 Students can be assigned into paired teams from the outset, which will accelerate the feedback cycle from the beginning of the process. Also, students can engage in *Thinking Aloud* with a parent, other teachers, or community members as part of a homework assignment where they not only work through the assigned problem, but then report on their discourse and thought processes.

 This strategy ties in nicely with *Strategy 8: Parents on Board*, especially if students are encouraged to discuss problem solving with their parents, siblings, or family members. Another strategy that pairs well with *Thinking Aloud* is *Strategy 13: Clear and Unclear Windows*; students can indicate what isn't clear, craft a question about what isn't clear, and then outline a plan for unearthing the solution to the questions they have.

From the Classroom

Meg Stengele is engaging students in reading and discussing *Lord of the Flies* as a part of their tenth grade English course. This book is very popular among students, yet Meg has struggled to get her students to think more deeply about the layers of meaning suggested by characterization, tone, and theme. She decided to try out *Think Aloud* with her students as they began reading the novel to help them generate some ideas as well as to work through to deeper contextual meanings and subplots within the book. Meg decided to use a "speed dating" setup where students reflect with a different partner at the close of each lesson, taking about five minutes per day. As the novel is read close to the start of the year, she hopes that this reflective assessment will also help students get to know one another, so this particular structuring for *Think Aloud* serves two purposes: content knowledge and socialization of the students.

Here are some sample questions that Meg Stengele used for her prompts:

What do you think about the rules (or lack of rules) that are present for the boys?

What would you have done when Jack asserted his leadership so forcefully?

Is Piggy right or wrong in his approach to thinking through problems? Why?

What do you think will happen next? Explain.

Think back over the events from the previous chapters. Do the series of events remind you of anything that we have studied about in social studies? How so or not so?

What does this book tell you about human nature? Explain.

Students would *Think Aloud* with their partner for the last five minutes of class each day. As part of their homework, students would then write down a more developed reflection that incorporated both their individual thoughts and those of their partner. Meg discovered that following *Think Aloud* activities, students would arrive to class the following day with some truly amazing insights that drove their discussions into deeper and more thoughtful territory. This allowed her the opportunity to enrich their novel study by helping them forge connections to other pieces of literature and/ or history.

What Is Learning?

Education is a social process. Education is growth. Education is not preparation for life; education is life itself.
— John Dewey

John Dewey observed that school improves when the teacher becomes a learner and learners become teachers. Often we hear insightful teachers speak about how much they *learn* from their students. In some cases they may be speaking about content or subject matter, and more often probably about the students themselves. A teacher learns new things every day. In his book, *Small Is Beautiful*, E.F. Schumacher (1973) notes that even animals teach us. He points out how much someone learns from a pet cat or dog, a cow, or other domestic animal. We learn lessons of responsibility, caring, nurture, and most of all patience. At least the potential to learn these things is there. So why would a teacher *not* learn much of value from his or her students?

The Roman orator Seneca wrote that "we learn best by teaching." This is so because if we must teach something, we now have an additional, more compelling, reason for learning it. We argue in this book that learning should be active, that it is a pursuit. If students are making robots from Legos, that is active. If they are putting on a play or puppet show, that, too, is active. But even such traditionally "passive" work as reading and listening should be active. Active learning shifts the center of gravity from the "teacher" to the learner. Economist Peter Drucker (1990), writing about schools, concluded that nothing much is going to change until schools are willing to cross the frontier from teaching to learning. Drucker's perceptive comment informs us that the best results will happen when the responsibility for learning lies directly with the learner. The learner must take ownership.

Learning Community Discussion Starters

1. Good teachers are learners by nature. They like challenges. How can you make your classroom a more reflective place for yourself and your students?

2. Think about a time you learned something of value; maybe how you learned to read or learned to ride a bicycle. What was it like? How were you different as a result?

Strategy 3
The Week in Review

If I am to speak for ten minutes, I need a week for preparation.
— President Woodrow Wilson

Purpose

The Week in Review (TWR) is a collaborative activity in which students assess the classroom events and activities of the week. The idea of *TWR* is similar to that of the television program *Washington Week in Review*, in which several talking heads sit together, each offering his or her perspective on the significant national and international events of the week. The heart of the matter is a discussion of the implications and meaning of those events. The difference is that your students will discuss the major happenings of the week in the classroom, or, in some cases, at school in general, as they experienced them.

Procedure

TWR typically takes approximately twenty minutes and is best conducted on a Friday. To maximize participation, it is advantageous to ask each student to take five minutes or so to work alone, making a list of what the student thinks were the three or four most significant ideas, activities, experiences, and the like, of the week at school. With a written list in hand, a student is far more likely to contribute to the discussion because the student has been afforded an opportunity to give the matter some prior thought. This also provides a level of structure often missing in student small-group interaction.

Each member of the group is given the opportunity to share his or her ideas, and then the discussion begins. The challenge for each group is to come to some agreement on the significant events of the week and to prepare a list to be reported to the class and turned in to you. In a typical classroom, this means that eight to ten group lists will be generated. This will give you the luxury of having a large number of thoughtful perspectives on what your class thinks was significant. Procedures such as *TWR* can go a long way in reducing the gap between what important things the teacher thinks are being taught and what important things students think they are learning. This represents the pursuit of the practical in classroom life; it is a search for understanding.

The ideal group size for this activity is three or four students. This provides multiple perspectives while allowing each group member a chance to share. Research* in small-group interaction consistently shows that for purposes of participation by all members the optimum group sizes are two, three, or, at most, four. When groups are larger, certain members withdraw from active participation, and one or two members dominate. If you use a group size of four, we suggest that you assign one group member the role of moderator, whose task it is to be sure that the other three members are each invited to contribute to the discussion.

Outcomes

TWR serves several purposes. First, students are encouraged to reflect on what they have done in the past several days and on the significance of the activities in which they have participated. What was important? What were some key ideas? What have we learned that has some significance? What was enjoyable? What could have been improved? This is the beginning of the search for meaning.

Second, your students' sense of what was meaningful is something for you to compare with your own sense of what you tried to accomplish this week. What were the key ideas you tried to get across? What did you think was significant about the activities when you planned for them? To what extent did you achieve your objectives? What do *you* think were the highlights of the week?

Third, the student review gives you a good place to begin on the following Monday by using it to connect what went before to where you think things ought to be going. A persistent problem in teaching and learning is the lack of connectedness between and among lessons. Too often, each lesson appears to be an island of instruction, an event unto itself. *TWR* gives you and your students a port of entry for the new week based on last week's learning. In fact, a good way to start Monday morning is by summarizing what the students had to say in their analyses.

---

* Ellis, A. K. (2011). *Teaching and Learning Elementary Social Studies,* 9th edition. Boston, MA: Pearson Education.

Differentiating *The Week in Review*

 By using an active board or other interactive whiteboard device, students can share their thinking with each group having a slide on which to record their thinking. Different groups could come up and record their information and report to their peers while doing so. These slides could be saved and published for students to do some followup writing as homework (i.e., students go to the teacher's website to download the different group thoughts and use that as a basis for a writing assignment). Another way to have students record thinking is for groups to each be at a computer station where they create a document, Power Point slides, or other electronic media. These are then e-mailed to the teacher for review.

 When assigning groups for this activity, ensure that struggling students have a grouping that works best for them. Sometimes this grouping looks like a struggling student being paired with a stronger "buddy," whereas at other times it may be best for the struggling students to be grouped together so as to provide a forum where the student cannot shy away from the task at hand. Teachers must be vigilant to the needs of students and their placement into groups to ensure that maximal participation takes place.

Another way to help struggling students is to provide more context or direction for their discussion prior to the individual thinking time. By doing this, students already have the hint of a path which they can then follow and flesh out on their own.

 Students can put their individual thoughts or questions on sticky notes, and affix those individual thoughts to a sheet of butcher paper that is then used by the group to record the group's thinking and discussion regarding the week's activities. It is a simple way to quickly illuminate both individual and group thought processes.

Another way to keep this technique simple is to direct students to focus on a particular strand or element that framed the week's instruction. The teacher can propose that individual and group comments stick to the poem, book, or story that is being read in class, or for students to frame their discussion around connections to a larger "world theme." For example, if the class is studying the Cold War, and specifically talked about disarmament during the week, their comments about content or school would be made as part of the larger context of how the specific topic that week ties into the larger Cold War focus.

 Group thinking can be pushed much further if that group knows their work will be assessed and reviewed by both the teacher and their peers. Once groups have completed their week in review comments, those comments can be posted up in the room using butcher paper or electronic means (e.g., computer screen or ActivBoard). Then a "walking discussion" in which students write questions or clarifying comments on the work produced by their peer groups can take place. This can be concluded with a full-group discussion about similarities, differences, and questions or concerns that result from the discussion and debriefing. This particular approach allows students to see the myriad "important elements" from the week as perceived by themselves, their friends, and others in the room, thereby broadening their perspective.

 This strategy could be combined with *Strategy 10: I Can Teach*, with students leading a review session of main themes, ideas, or concepts, doing their week in review as a lesson plan for the teaching segment.

From the Classroom

David Voyager has found that middle school students tend to need more structure when doing reflective assessment activities. As a social studies teacher who tries to help students forge "big picture" connections, David likes the idea of a weekly review of learning, but he worries that students might not be able to draw connections spanning several days. He has adapted *The Week in Review* in such a way as to help his students tie together their daily learning to craft a big picture summary of what they have been doing. Each day, prior to leaving the classroom, the students hand David a slip of paper with what they thought the "big idea" for the day was.

On the last day of the week or unit, David stimulates the thinking of his students by displaying all of the big ideas contributed by students throughout the week or unit (he uses a variety of means ranging from butcher paper to a projection system). He groups students into groups of three or four for their *The Week in Review* discussion, ensuring that each group member has a specific task or duty. He assigns each group the task of finding a way to tie in as many of the big ideas as possible into one overarching theme or idea that would summarize the week's learning. The students name their theme and cite their supporting evidence (several of the listed big ideas) as rationale for their theme. As a group they turn in a document with their information; this document takes a different form each time, ranging from an idea web to a developed outline. David is then able to take the group's work to connect to the following week or use the group's work as a springboard to a larger writing assignment for that particular unit of study.

Finally, sometimes David writes his own *The Week in Review* and shares it with his students. He's found that it helps students see his intent in teaching concepts and sometimes it highlights gaps in knowledge for himself or his students. David has discovered that reviewing *The Week in Review* with the full class also lets him and his students see how different people might experience the same event in a different way, which has led to richer conversations about reflection and learning.

Necessary Conditions

Freedom of expression is the matrix, the indispensable condition.
— Benjamin Nathan Cardozo

The work of psychologist Carl Rogers (1969, 1983, 1994) is helpful to teachers who wish to create a participatory, honest, open, reflective environment. Rogers described several necessary conditions of classroom life. He made it clear that teachers need to work diligently on the development of these priorities. He never suggested that this is an easy task, and like most things worth doing it takes time. Here are the basic conditions:

♦ A climate of trust

The first priority is to *develop a climate of trust*. Many children and adolescents have learned not to trust others, especially adults. This is unfortunate but true. You can begin to address this problem through a conscious effort to model trust in your classroom. The teacher inevitably sets the tone. As your students experience your trust of them, the atmosphere will change in a positive way, not necessarily miraculously, but it does begin to change. An absence of trust breeds shame and intolerance; trust breeds openness and caring.

♦ Participatory decision making

John Dewey described school at its best as a miniature democracy. Democracy works best when well-informed citizens share in decisions. Think of your students as citizens who participate in the commonweal. The notion of the student who works alone, who offers little or nothing to the group but does reasonably good work, is inadequate in this context. Active participation in classroom life is crucial if the social/moral fabric of school life is to improve.

Richard Spady (2008) writes that every decision made in an organization (think classroom) should be made at the most primary or basic level possible. In a school context, this means teachers should turn over most of the decisions to students just as principals should turn over most decisions to teachers. The reason for this is that there is no other way to establish a participatory environment of decision making. Those organizations that work best, whether they are businesses, governments, or schools, are those that have learned that democracy is not an abstraction but something to be practiced daily. A place to start is with everyday classroom life.

- ♦ Self-respect

    A third priority is to *help students prize themselves.* Psychologist Ellen Langer (1998) makes a powerful distinction between self-esteem and self-respect. She notes that trouble follows when we attempt to cultivate self-esteem. Self-esteem is an evaluative idea that focuses on what others might think of us. Even people with high self-esteem are caught in an evaluative framework. It is not unusual, for example, for convicted felons to have high self-esteem. Self-respect, on the other hand, means accepting who we are, liking ourselves, and even being aware of our limitations without undue worry. By treating your students with respect, by treating them with dignity whatever their ability, you model a major contribution to their own sense and acceptance of who they are. Respect for others is contagious. Watch it spread in your classroom.

- ♦ Sociable scholarship and emotional excitement

    A fourth condition of a reflective classroom is that the teacher *models the excitement of intellectual and emotional discovery.* This condition implies two things. First, the teacher must be an enthusiastic learner. Second, the teacher must be a relational person. If you put the two together, great things happen. A caring teacher who loves learning is a powerful presence in a classroom.

Let's consider an example or two for purposes of illustration. If you teach reading, then one behavior you can start with is to raise your profile as a reader. This means that you must do a great deal of reading, especially of high-quality books, and that you must share what you are learning with your students. Tell them about ideas, challenges, characters, themes, descriptions, and the like. By the way, it is also eminently worthwhile to share samples of good word choice and syntax by a gifted writer with your students. Beyond that you might share how you take notes when you read, especially when you are struck by a profound idea or way of saying something.

If you are teaching history, let the students see some of the "historian" in you. Tell them about your own visits to museums. Share some of your own historical interests, whether in the reading you do, your hobbies and collections, places you have been, what you find interesting, or some of your specific interests related to historical topics. It really is as simple as that.

If you want to model an even higher level of intellectual excitement and inquiry, step across subject-matter boundaries. Curiously, even in elementary school, this is rarely done, but when it does happen, students begin to see a whole world of connections. Here are some examples: The mathematics teacher who talks about a visit to an art museum; the music teacher who takes some time to demonstrate the physics of music by teaching students about oscillations, sympathetic vibration, and harmonics; the primary teacher who tells the students about the wonderful class he or she is taking in order to learn more about teaching.

It has been said that all true learning engages the emotions. People learn best when they *feel* some sense of excitement about what they are doing. The attitude is one of "I can't wait to get started on this project" or "I know the kids are going to love this." Typically when this level of excitement is caught by the students, it manifests itself in such comments as, "Do we have to put away our stuff already?" or "Can we keep working on this tomorrow?" These are the kinds of comments that make teaching worthwhile.

Conclusion

The necessary conditions of classroom life that we have addressed here are rather simple. But they are significant. If you implement them, you will experience a changed environment, one that is at once more intellectually, socially, and morally satisfying and profound. Do you want to be remembered by your students? Here is what you must do: First, maintain a well-regulated participatory environment; second, be enthusiastic about learning; and third, show the kids you care about them.

Learning Community Discussion Starters

1. Benjamin Cardozo stated that, "Freedom of expression is the matrix, the indispensable condition." What does this mean for life in classrooms? What connections exist between freedom of expression and the process of learning?

2. What are some barriers to putting the "necessary conditions" into practice in your own classroom? What are some steps you can take to overcome these barriers?

Strategy 4
Post It Up

Posters of the sea and land, thus do go about, about.
— William Shakespeare

In Colonial America, there were people known as pamphleteers who attempted to get their ideas across by distributing and posting notices. The most famous of these was Thomas Paine, a leader of the American independence movement. His pamphlet, *Common Sense*, served to stir the heart of many a Colonist. Martin Luther used a similar technique in 1517 when he posted his famous *95 Theses* on the door of the church in Wittenburg, Germany. At a less consequential level, just walk through a neighborhood on a spring day and count the posted notices of yard sales, meetings, and the like. The posting of notices is a time-honored means of communication.

The *Post It Up** strategy is designed to afford students and teachers opportunities to make public their ideas and opinions. The commentary should be brief enough to write on a Post-it note or a small square piece of paper. It's an old way to communicate, but it works. *Post It Up* communicates without necessarily talking or directly engaging others. If a student has an idea or suggestion to make, the student can write it down on the note and place it in some reasonable spot in the room. If the message is simply one of encouragement from one student to another, then the note can be placed on the recipient's desktop. It is actually a low-tech version of e-mail.

A primary use of *Post It Up* is as a kind of ubiquitous suggestion box. When students are working on projects or doing problem solving, thoughts will occur to them of a nature that does not demand the interrupting of the group or others at the time. There will be time enough later to take up the suggestion. By having a place to store and post ideas, we ensure that they will not be lost.

It is common for students to be disciplined for passing notes during class time. A reasonable question is, "Why do they do it?" Typically, the answer is that they wish to communicate something to someone else without necessarily drawing everyone else's attention to that fact. This is a *problem* waiting to be turned into a *solution*. Why not encourage students to communicate

---

* We are indebted to N.J. Petersen, who suggested the idea for this strategy.

this way? If you have created the kind of classroom environment that supports student-to-student communication, builds trust, and encourages connections, then you need not be overly worried that their attempts to communicate with each other will be primarily devious, off task, and destructive of learning.

Outcomes

Post It Up is particularly useful if you are attempting to create an atmosphere of civility, respect, and mutual support. A note of encouragement from a teacher or a fellow student goes a long way toward making people feel welcome, involved, and encouraged. *Post it Up* gives students an ongoing opportunity to take the initiative in this regard.

Can it be overdone? It can be. Personally, we would rather err on the side of too many ideas, notes of encouragement, and supportive statements than too few. Can it turn into a negative thing? Yes, it can. But whatever it turns out to be will reflect the underlying social and moral conditions that have been cultivated in the classroom. Therefore, we are assuming that this will not be something to give you undue concern. And if a certain number of the notes are negative in tone, then you have a *real*, not a contrived issue to discuss with your class, itself an opportunity for problem solving and reflective thought.

Differentiating *Post It Up*

 Student groups can be put in charge of a particular element or topic for the discussion, where they craft the question and then monitor the followup on the responses that are written and posted. Another variation on a theme is to have students "pro vs. con" on different questions where one student takes one viewpoint while another plays devil's advocate. Their written discussion might stimulate thoughts for other students about the topic.

 Blogging is a natural way to incorporate this strategy in an electronic setting, as is the use of online discussion forums or discussion threads. Teachers can post a question (or even require students to craft and post questions) on a regular basis and have a portion of student grades be based on meaningful contributions to those forums or threads. This is easily done both in class or during the student's own time.

 Record Keeping (Strategy 15) works great with this strategy, especially if it is done electronically as most blogs or discussion forms allow the administrator (the teacher) to track the contributions of each participant as well as to track how much time participants are reading the posts that have been made.

From the Classroom

Den Mauk teaches an integrated Humanities class that encompasses both English and social studies curriculum in a two-hour block. As a part of their studies, students engage in a variety of interdisciplinary activities. Den was uncertain of how to help students demonstrate their mastery of concepts or ideas when he came across the *Post It Up* reflective assessment. Den started this activity by introducing the space to the students and explaining to them that it would be their space to use as they saw fit. A classroom discussion was held to establish some ground rules for what could or could not be posted in the space.

Students decided to theme the space in a way to line up with what they were studying in class, which Den says has been a great value-added part of his classroom learning environment. Sometimes the theme is more history oriented, while other times the theme is based on a piece of literature or a literary concept that the students are studying. Every two weeks another student maintains "ownership" of the Post It Up space. The student in charge puts up new backing. The students determine the theme for the space and indicate that theme with a catchy title. During the two weeks following, students write in comments, ask questions, post solutions to class work, and even display their theme-related artwork.

Here is what Den's students had to say about their Post It Up space:

I am pretty shy and afraid of what others might say. But one day I wrote up my idea on the Post It Up board, and lots of other students commented on how great it was. That was really cool!

Mr. Mauk said that the Post It Up board would go away if students weren't using it. Well, I don't think it is going anywhere anytime soon. It is always full of questions, thoughts, comments, and cool stuff. I especially like when we post up our solutions to problems or our artwork.

Lots of times my friends or I come in during lunch or before school to put information up there or to post up a relevant article or cartoon that they found in the paper. It's neat to have a place where we make our own connections between what we're learning and our lives without Mr. Mauk telling us what the connections should be.

I think Mr. Mauk was kinda nervous about us having a Post It Up space. I was maybe nervous too, that perhaps some other kids might write things that weren't nice or appropriate. But so far, it's been a really great part of our room and people are being very supportive and positive. It's my favorite part of the classroom.

I enjoy being able to express my ideas with a cartoon or picture! It's also awesome to see other students commenting on my work and giving me (and other kids) compliments about our posts.

What Is Assessment?

I watched the child without interrupting her, and counted how many time she would do her work over and over.

— Maria Montessori

There is a small minority of educators who oppose *any* formal attempts to assess school learning. Their position is basically that such efforts erode trust and other relational qualities between teachers and students. Students are told, they note, to learn for the joy of learning, and just about the time they take us seriously, we destroy the experience by testing them. Furthermore, they cite the damage done to the self-image of those who do poorly on tests. Is it worth it, they ask, to hurt people in the name of finding out what they know? There is definitely something to these criticisms. As critics of formal testing so often point out, school is the only place in the world where you have to be tested so often, so publicly, and so artificially.

Many students and teachers view tests as separate events, set apart from learning and teaching. This is, in fact, the traditional model of assessment. We've all heard the dire warning, "Don't forget, the test will be on Friday," or something to that effect. Young children, who tend to view the world as a whole, not as a collection of parts, are especially confused with formal testing procedures. After all, they have been busy learning to do real things like riding bicycles and learning the rules of games, important things, without being subjected to paper-and-pencil tests over what they've learned.

Why all the need for assessment? We really think it is a fair question for students and teachers to consider and discuss. To assess because we've always done it is not a sufficient reason. We want to give you some reasons why we should assess teaching and learning, but before we get into them, we do need to make one thing clear: The more you can bring teaching, learning, and assessment together, the more successful you and your students will become in knowing how and to what extent meaningful progress is being made.

Some reasons for assessing teaching and learning are as follows:

♦ To classify students

One reason for assessing student achievement is to *classify* or *grade* students. Whether or not it is a compelling reason is debatable; nevertheless, one job of the schools is to determine who has learned sufficiently to be awarded promotions, diplomas, entrance to university, and the like. Without such information we simply could not sort students on the basis of their achievements. Terms like excellence, mediocrity, and failure would have no school-related meaning.

♦ To diagnose students

A second reason is *diagnostic*. Without some means of assessment, we would have no way of making meaningful referrals to remedial, gifted, or other programs. Diagnosis is often used to place students in situations where their academic needs are best met. We mention later in this book (see *Strategy 13: Clear and Unclear Windows*) that we only wish we were as interested in assessing student strengths as we are in assessing their weaknesses!

♦ To encourage and support learning

A third reason for assessment is to *encourage and support student progress.* Most of us want to know from time to time how we are doing. We would like to know that we can do certain things better, that we know more about something, that our insights have deepened. One way in which we can have some assurance of these matters is to document our growth through some means of record keeping (see *Strategy 15: Record Keeping*) and assessment. Diagnosis gives us some idea, however rough, of where we are, and assessment at the end of an experience gives us some idea of how far we've come. But ongoing assessment, particularly by the students themselves, creates awareness and has the potential to offer a support system for learning. In other words, the purpose of assessment in this context is self-knowledge and feedback.

We don't mean to minimize these reasons. Formal testing is part of the culture. However, our focus in this book is on a rationale for assessment that integrates it with teaching and learning. In that sense, our concern is with small-scale reflective assessment as a seamless part of classroom life. So, please consider the student self-assessment as inseparable from teaching and learning in a world where all three come together naturally.

The best assessment is that which leads to the improvement of individuals and groups. Without this perspective, there is little hope of excellence. If a child is a mediocre speller and has the potential and desire to become a good speller, we ought to do what we can to make it happen. If a student is a great natural musician, one who loves music, the question becomes, "What can we do to provide challenging opportunities for that student?" If a group of students is struggling with a performance and we can document some reasons why that is so, we ought to act decisively to improve things. In each case, the best assessment will be a combination of expert judgment and input from the person(s) affected.

Beneath the desire and the means to improve, however, there is another issue, one that is often not addressed. That issue is one of meaning, purpose, and truth. After all, given proper diagnosis and expert help with needed skills, a person could become a better thief, so improvement alone is not sufficient. When assessment is left at the level of technical skills and interests, there is no compelling moral matrix, no redeeming social purpose. One could argue that we would not attempt to teach anything that is not morally and socially uplifting, so only good skills are taught and learned at school. Even if this were the case, there is still an obligation to find out whether students know this for sure.

Seamless teaching, learning, and assessment occur when teachers make the following commitments to classroom life:

- ◆ Create a climate of openness and enthusiasm;

- ◆ Desire to learn and share learning;

- ◆ Relationship of meaning to action;

- ◆ Individual and group reflection as expected practice; and

- ◆ True freedom of speech and action.

Conclusion

In reality, there are three worlds of assessment. Each has its proper place. The first world is *technical*; it deals with *how to*. The technical level is goal directed, feedback-controlled, and mainly behavioral. Many teachers seem to be willing to stop at this level, going no further. The second level is the *practical* level where communication is emphasized along with a sense of others, and teaching and learning as a *social activity*. The teachers who reach this level accomplish remarkable things with their students. The third level is *reflective*; it is a world of freedom and empowerment. This very rare level ought to be the long-term goal to which you aspire. Freedom of speech and action, feelings of empowerment, and an atmosphere of transcendence and esprit de corps are the outcomes.

Learning Community Discussion Starters

1. What would a classroom be like where the commitments listed above become reality?

2. The Latin root word *asidere* literally means to "sit with." This is the word from which assessment derives some of its meaning. In what ways can educators "sit with" their students and assess their learning? What are some of the moral implications of "sitting with" students as part of an overall assessment process?

Strategy 5

Jigsaw

We must try to trust one another. Stay and cooperate.
— Jomo Kenyatta

Purpose

The *Jigsaw* strategy, developed by the eminent psychologist Elliot Aronson (2009), is an example of cooperative learning that contains within it an individualistic goal structure. The idea of *Jigsaw* is that each student in a cooperative learning group of, say, three students is responsible for peer teaching his or her companions a portion of the material that they all need to learn. Thus each student "teaches" one-third of the information, skills, or whatever, and is "taught" two-thirds of the content. It is important that students do their best to teach their peers well because all the members of a group are depending on each other. This has the potential to create a truly reflective environment in which students accept responsibility for helping each other learn.

Procedure

When a *Jigsaw* group of students is assembled, it is crucial that each member has something tangible to contribute. This means preparation, an important step in any problem-solving process. The idea is that each student becomes an "expert" in one part of a whole task. So, if students are learning about the three states (liquid, solid, gas) of water, each student in a jigsaw group is assigned to inform the others about the properties of water in a particular state.

We recommend that in most cases you require students to write down clear notes or points they wish to cover during the group meeting. Any materials or illustrations also should be assembled in advance. This way, when the group comes together, the time is spent productively. Because you will typically have three students in a group, you will have to make it clear that each person should be given equal time to present. Of course, you should allow a few minutes for each group to converse informally, a sort of "warmup" time, and you should allow time at the conclusion of the presentations for the group to do some reflective thinking about what they have learned.

There is an intermediate step that can greatly contribute to the success of the *Jigsaw* strategy. For example, if the topic is the plot of a novel by chapter, Step 1 is for each student to prepare his or her part of the presentation to the group. Step 2 brings students together (perhaps in groups of five to keep things manageable) who have studied the same thing. They are able to check with each other for accuracy, ideas, procedures, and the like. This intermediate step helps to ensure more accurate presentations, and it gives each student a kind of rehearsal prior to his or her presentation. So, to return to our topic of chapter-by-chapter plot analysis, the students who studied the first few chapters will meet together briefly, as will those who studied middle chapters and those who studied the closing chapters. When students complete Step 2, they are ready to rejoin their *Jigsaw* groups. In Step 3, the groups come together and teach each other so that all important points are covered. But keep in mind that in a class of thirty students, there is the potential for three groups of ten students to have each studied the same part of the lesson.

Outcomes

Jigsaw is included among the reflective strategies for bringing teaching, learning, and assessment together because peer teaching is one of the best ways for students to learn and to become conscious of what they are learning. It is both teaching and learning at once. Jean Piaget concluded that children are more effective than most adults realize in teaching each other, especially if teachers provide some structure and support. This is so, Piaget claimed, because of a language issue, namely that greater syntactic compatibility is found within the peer group than exists when, for example, adults talk to children.

Example: The American Revolution

The Boston Tea Party, the Battle of Lexington, and Paul Revere's Ride are three events that led up to the American Revolution. Using the *Jigsaw* strategy, each student in a group of three takes one of the events and studies it thoroughly. After students have had the opportunity to study their respective events, the Boston Tea Party students meet together to share what they have learned. So do the Battle of Lexington students and the Paul Revere's Ride students.

Now the *Jigsaw* groups are convened, and students take turns teaching their peers. You need to coach your students in techniques for making the information they present interesting, significant, and engaging. These are small groups of three, composed of an "expert" in each of the three historical events. Their task is to teach each other.

A variant form is for one-third of the class to be assigned the Boston Tea Party, one-third to be assigned the Battle of Lexington, and one-third to be assigned Paul Revere's ride. Each group studies its particular topic and prepares a skit, booklet, maps, drawings, literature, and other materials, and is given time to "teach" the other students. This makes three presentations with a high degree of student involvement, and it combines two strategies: *Jigsaw* and *I Can Teach* (Strategy 10).

Differentiating *Jigsaw*

 One way to incorporate technology into this great strategy is to use multiple document cameras. When the students assemble into the second round of *Jigsaw* groups wherein the various subject experts are sharing their unique information, each student presenter can write up his or her information for his or her peers and have it displayed on the document camera for the group. That way, there is a group record of the top information from each segment of presentation. This also would allow for groups to compare the "essential information" that was shared out in the second round of *Jigsaw* and double-check that each group did, in fact, receive similar information across the board.

 Having a "study buddy" for special needs students helps the student with learning difficulties gain confidence in their acquisition of knowledge and presentation of information. By pairing up special needs students with a peer, the peer can help that student with presenting or sharing information in both rounds of *Jigsaw* activities. As the year progresses and the students become comfortable with this technique, you will find that those students who once needed a buddy are now comfortable presenting and sharing on their own!

 Jigsaw can be made quicker and easier by making groups smaller. You can double up on the assignment of topic groups and have smaller sharing groups. This speeds up the process exponentially, yet still allows for inquiry learning and student presentation of information (i.e., student-centered learning).

 Jigsaw can be made much more comprehensive and difficult by preassigning students areas to research and giving them a great deal of free reign on their assigned topics. This gives students the experience of culling research information to the salient points worthy of sharing in a discussion. Students could be given a class period (or be assigned as homework) to find all of the research information on their topic in the library or via an online research database. Then students would meet in their topic groups, and all students would have a wealth of information for sharing, so they would need to really pare down to the essentials, building their skill of prioritizing information for presentation purposes. Another way to dig deeper with *Jigsaw* is to have students create a visual or write a paper on what they learned and how they would prioritize the different elements. They could also incorporate a reflective paragraph on their learning processes.

 This strategy can be easily integrated with *I Learned* (Strategy 1) statements, in which students reflect on how they learned and what they learned. *Clear and Unclear Windows* (Strategy 13) is also a natural fit. Using that strategy, students share what makes sense as well as indicating areas of concern or areas with unresolved questions. Finally, *I Can Teach* (Strategy 10) is embedded in this strategy, so a brief review of how that strategy works might enhance both teacher and student experiences while using *Jigsaw*.

From the Classroom

Britt McJacob wanted her students to gain a deeper insight into the many causes of World War I, a complex series of events with which students often struggle. She had previously used direct instruction for this, as it afforded her the ability to get through a lot of content in short order. However, she discovered that student retention of the information was minimal at best and completely absent at worst. She was searching for a creative way to have students learn the information in a deeper yet efficient way when she found the *Jigsaw*.

Britt grouped her students into ten groups of three, and had each group research a different cause of World War I. The groups were instructed to have all students in the group have the same information in their notes by the time their conversations ended. The groups also developed a five-minute presentation about their material that each of the students could deliver independently. The next day, Britt had her students rearrange themselves into three larger groups of ten, with each group having a representative from each of the causes of the war. The students in the new groups took turns presenting their information while their peers listened and wrote down the information.

Following the group-sharing period, Britt led the group in a discussion about significance of the various causes. She had students talk about cause and effect and make some predictions about what would happen, using *Jigsaw* information as the basis of their rationale. Britt also had students discern which causes might have played a more significant role than others, again using their discussion information to provided the basis of their thinking.

Britt shared that "the kids seemed to be much more involved in the teaching and learning of the causes when we used *Jigsaw*, whereas before it seemed like I was pulling teeth to keep their attention. I also notice that the quality of their written notes was better. I'm not sure why that is, but I am thinking it might be because their peers put the information into 'teenager friendly' terminology, thereby leading to them understanding the information and getting it down on paper more efficiently."

As a reflective closure for the discussion, Britt had students do a word cluster where students illustrated the significance of various causes by the amount of space each cause took on the page. She took these word clusters and displayed them, and then used them as the basis of a class discussion later in the week.

Two Goals of School Life

The foundation of education is to raise children to be fine human beings.

— Shinichi Suzuki

People who set a limited number of strategically significant goals are generally far more successful in goal attainment than those who either have no stated goals or who have too many goals to track. This is true in politics, business, child rearing, school, and any other walk of life. The keys are to have a limited number of goals, be certain that the goals you do have are worth believing in, and establish concrete ways of realizing the goals.

We propose only two goals of school life. We are convinced that if you take these two goals seriously, you will see positive, lasting, tangible results. If we limit ourselves to two goals, several things become possible. First, it is easy to keep track of two goals. Secondly, it is relatively easy to communicate such a limited number of goals to students, parents, and other interested parties. And third, when it comes to measuring goal attainment, wouldn't you rather have two goals to measure rather than the typical dozen or so? What we are proposing is that we not get lost in the goal structure, which is more often than not exactly what happens.

The two goals we propose are as follows:

♦ Raising everyone's academic achievement

♦ Improving the social/moral fabric of classroom life

This is all you need. You do not need a laundry list of aims, objectives, goal statements, and the like. Keep it simple. Make sure every student and every student's parents know the goals.

Let's examine the first goal: *raising academic achievement*. You may be teaching in an environment where test scores are already high, or in an environment where the present situation is something less than that. The point is that we can always do better no matter who we are. This is true for each individual. High achievers, middle achievers, and low achievers all can—and should—improve their academic work. This is not meant in a competitive sense. It merely means that you, us, and others can always read better literature, learn more mathematics, and become more aware of the world in which we live. Psychologist Albert Bandura's (1971, 2005) *Social Learning Theory* posits that people learn from observation, imitation, and modeling. It is an awesome task to be a teacher because you are living what you teach as you are on display as a model to the kids.

The second goal is *improving the social/moral fabric of school life.* In a classroom, crowded, uncomfortable conditions typically are the norm. Most teachers would prefer to have a larger room, more space for the students to work, a little privacy, and more places to put things. We know from experience that it isn't easy. In spite of these real limitations, the social/moral fabric improves when there is civility, collaboration, freedom of expression, a sense of responsibility to others, and when each person's dignity is respected. These are not abstract ideas. They represent the simple, tangible elements of an improved social/moral fabric. Think of your classroom as a system. In any system, the base must be anchored with a few reasonable rules for it to work. And the system must be open enough to allow freedom of expression and movement and to make each person welcome. Again, Bandura's (1971, 2005) *Social Learning Theory* comes to mind. Your behaviors are on display.

The two strategic goals are inseparable. The more you practice the strategies contained in this book, the more we think you will agree with this idea. Academic achievement without morality is not merely hollow, it is dangerous. Morality without academic achievement leaves us with a weak excuse for having school, one that the public will not and should not accept.

Conclusion

The key to bringing these two strategic goals of school life into sync is reflective practice. A reflective classroom is by definition a place where the two goals are being taken seriously by all involved. Teaching, learning, and assessment together in the context of reflective practice is our theme. The two goals are practical, attainable goals in almost any given school situation. As you build up the connections between teaching, learning, and assessment, and as you and your students search for significance and meaning in the life of your classroom, two things will happen: First, academic achievement will rise, and second, your classroom will become a more civil, responsible, and moral place in which to work and play.

Learning Community Discussion Starters

1. Social learning theory states that students learn from us through observation, imitation, and modeling. What are the teaching/learning implications of this well-researched conclusion?

2. It is argued that the recent standards movement has focused too heavily on raising academic achievement to the exclusion of other educational goals. How do you feel about this?

Strategy 6
Key Idea Identification

We always advance slowly from one sensible idea to another….
— Jean-Jacques Rousseau

Purpose

Philosopher Alfred North Whitehead (1929) wrote that "the first thing to do with an idea is to prove it." What he meant by "prove" an idea is to "prove its worth." Whitehead takes his place among many great educational thinkers who are convinced that the "coverage" approach to teaching and learning is intellectually unproductive. His advice to teachers was, "do not teach too many subjects,…and what you teach, teach thoroughly." Essentially, he is saying that key ideas have staying power and that they should be carefully chosen and carefully emphasized by teachers. He points us gently toward the *quality* of the experience, not the quantity of material covered.

One way to think about the educational power of ideas is to consider what you'd like to have your students remember about a particular subject a year from now and into the future. You can test how well this worked for you. Recall your own second grade, sixth grade, eleventh grade, or whatever year. What ideas do you remember from a particular class? If the teacher was successful with the subject matter and the experience in general, you will remember two things: the feelings and the ideas. The feelings should be positive, and the ideas should be few but powerful.

Procedure

As an assessment strategy, *Key Idea Identification* asks students to thoughtfully consider a lesson or series of related activities and to specify what they think is the key idea, main theme, or concept. Here is how it works.

At the close of a lesson or activity, ask students to identify what they think was the main or key idea. Of course, it helps to hold discussions from time to time on such topics as "What is an idea?" "Are ideas and skills different, and if so, how?" "When you read a book or listen to a presentation, how can you tell ideas from information?" Don't be surprised if your students have never discussed such questions.

When you ask students to identify the key idea of a lesson, give them a little room to make interpretations. Their sense of the key idea may differ from yours. You don't need to fish for the "correct" answer. A good reflective session can happen after you have collected the impressions of your students and compare and contrast them with your own sense of the key idea.

A variation on the *Key Idea* strategy is to have students, in small groups of three, discuss their own perspectives on the key idea of a lesson just completed. This provides them with the opportunity to *Think Aloud* (Strategy 2) as they reflect on the lesson and separate the wheat from the chaff. In addition to identifying the key idea, students should be asked to explain why this is the key idea. It represents a review, but more than that—it is a review in search of *essence*. The quest is to figure out what is at the heart of the matter.

Outcomes

Several significant outcomes should occur from the search for key ideas. One outcome is aimed directly at the teacher. If you are going to have students identify the key idea of a lesson, it makes sense for you to have one in mind before you teach the lesson. Thus you can raise your own level of consciousness about what you are doing. John Goodlad (1984, 2004), in his classic educational book, *A Place Called School*, noted that he seldom encountered classroom situations where teachers were teaching ideas. Mainly, he said, they teach information and skills. Goodlad concluded that possibly teachers do not think ideas are important or perhaps they themselves do not think in terms of ideas. Neither thought is particularly encouraging and you and we need to do something about it.

If students are to be asked to consider the *Key Idea* of an activity or lesson, or even the key idea of the week as a whole, they, too, need to raise their level of consciousness. Your students will come to think of learning at its best as being composed of ideas. This is a good place to begin the processes of critical thinking, to consider how information can be put together to form knowledge, and how knowledge can serve as the foundation for ideas. This is the beginning of insight. Who knows but that in time it could lead to wisdom.

Finally, if teachers and students are actively looking for key ideas, then we have a clear signal that ideas are valued. This means that students need to think about the key idea(s) they wish to communicate in their writing, conversation, drawing, constructing, and other forms of expression. Thus teaching, learning, and reflective assessment come together to form a harmonious whole.

Differentiating *Key Idea Identification*

A variation on the *Key Idea* theme is to have students, in small groups of three, discuss their own perspectives on the key idea of a lesson just completed. This provides them an opportunity to think aloud as they reflect on the lesson and separate the wheat from the chaff. In addition to identifying the key idea, students should be asked to explain *why* this is the key idea. It represents a review, but more than that. It is a review in search of essence. The quest is to figure out what is at the heart of the matter. Student groups can also process the individual responses of peers.

Having the available text or content projected via document camera or on an interactive whiteboard offers students the ability to highlight specific text or concepts as they share their key idea with the group. If each student used a different pen color on the interactive whiteboard, you would then have a collection that shows points where student thinking converges or diverges, thereby stimulating further discussion.

Students can also blog their key ideas with their peers on an online discussion board or in an electronic classroom setting. Threads can allow students to discuss similarities and differences in thinking, bring in primary source documents to substantiate their thoughts, or cite literary sources from which their ideas are derived.

By focusing on the fact that there really is no wrong key idea, students feel less pressured to "get it right" and are brought into the activity. *Key Idea Identification* is a great strategy to help those students who struggle academically with understanding what an essential concept might be and why it is identified as such; by watching and hearing their peers discuss their individual key ideas students gain insights on how to prioritize information and content.

Start small and have students only identify one key idea for the first few times that you try this activity. A visual "web" diagram is a great way for students to branch out and make connections between the overall big idea and some of the supporting concepts from the past day or week of learning. This process can also be made simpler by having student use quotes from notes, text, literature, or class discussion as the key idea, rather than constructing their own from scratch.

The possibilities of this concept are truly limitless as students can forge meaningful connections in a variety of ways. Simply by asking for specific or more general identifications, the teacher can push student thinking to new heights! Have students craft their key idea without paraphrasing or quoting materials from class to see if they are able to synthesize learning at a deeper and more meaningful level. Students could also be prompted to craft their key idea as a thesis statement, and then to provide concrete details and commentary to support their choice. Key ideas could be shared among students using a "pyramid discussion" in reverse; they could start by identifying the key idea, talking about it, and then broadening the discussion to show their supporting evidence. This forces students to contextualize their key idea, as well as helps them provide some rationale for their choice. It provides excellent practice for persuasive or expository writing!

From the Classroom

Jaqueline Conners has been teaching students about the Age of Enlightenment. A main focus of this unit is the philosophers from that time period and their revolutionary ideas. Jaqueline is hoping that students will connect the philosophy postulated by Enlightenment thinkers with modern-day laws, civics, and ethics. As they conclude reading and discuss various philosophers, Jaqueline has students write down the key idea(s) of that particular philosopher and limits them to no more than three key ideas per class segment. Some examples of what students wrote are below:

> The whole idea of "man is free but everywhere he is in chains" underlies the idea of a law-driven society. I can't believe that this idea is so old!

> The first amendment is all Voltaire! He said that "I might disagree with what you say but will defend to the death your right to say it." That is the essence of freedom of speech.

> I realize that the founding fathers took a lot of pieces of ideas from a lot of different philosophers and then drew up our country based on those ideas. I see that by reading and researching you can take away the best thinking and ideas to create something even greater.

> Thoreau's idea about "natural law" really makes a lot of sense. The laws of natural consequences can really govern decisions of people, and to build laws based on those natural consequences makes total sense to me.

Jaqueline found that *Key Idea Identification* worked best when the key ideas were not really evaluated by her. The idea that there is no true right answer is something that actually motivates students to put out new and different thoughts that come about as a result of their learning. Jaqueline found that even if a student wrote "I can't think of a key idea," it was a sign that she and that student might do some brainstorming to further the student's thinking. Afterward, the student came up with some really applicable and creative thoughts.

Basic Life Skills and Career Success

This was my life—my life—my career, my brilliant career!
— Stella Maria Miles Franklin

In his pioneering research done in the 1970s, Harvard's David McClelland (1973) identified the crucial differences between the most and least successful people in the world of work. The most successful had three competencies that clearly distinguished them from the least successful:

♦ Empathy

♦ Self-discipline

♦ Initiative

McClellan's work clearly showed that when these qualities or competencies are present in an individual, the chances are very good indeed that he or she will do well in the world of work. And when they are lacking, even a high level of technical skill is not enough to make a person successful. Technical skills are important, to be sure, but they are not a reasonable substitute for caring about others, for taking responsibility, and for doing the right thing in ambiguous situations.

Furthermore, it is estimated that IQ and academic test results account for less than 25% of job success. Some estimates place it as low as 4%. If we take the higher figure, then 75% of job success comes from factors other than high test scores. The lower figure suggests that as much as 96% comes from other factors. Studies also show that the average American IQ has risen by 24 points since testing began in 1918, but a careful analysis by Achenbach, Dumenci, and Rescorla (2004) and by Achenbach, Howell, McConaughy, and Stanger (1998) shows "emotional intelligence," which is comprised of the three qualities mentioned above and a few other related attributes, on the decline. Further studies point to the need for individuals to possess the following qualities in life:

- *Team building:* A genuine desire to be a constructive part of group efforts, to build others up, to play whatever role is necessary for the good of the team.

- *Adaptability:* A willingness to accept ambiguity and uncertainty as part of life and to see opportunity in situations where not everything is clearly laid out.

- *Resilience:* The ability to bounce back, to not become easily discouraged when things are difficult, to work with persistence toward meaningful goals.

- *Optimism:* A sense of hope and a willingness to see the positive aspects of situations in the face of setbacks, a "don't give up and we will win" spirit.

These findings suggest that we must search for deeper levels of classroom experience in teaching, learning, and assessment based on self-awareness, appropriate expression, coherence, trust, initiative, and esprit de corps. All this clearly points to the need for collaborative work, group projects, team efforts, active learning, and an ongoing search for meaning in the things we do. The reason we must strive toward this in classrooms is because a student's career and adult life in general begins not in the workplace but in childhood and adolescent experience in working with others. As the poet William Wordsworth wrote, "the child is the father of the man." If we wish to prepare students for the complex world of the future, we are going to have to organize experiences that require conversation, group work, research skills, and adaptability.

For many teachers and students, this calls for readiness to change the routines of classroom life. In a nutshell, the change demands a more social environment. It means essentially abandoning the model of each student being "taught" in a group and working alone.

Conclusion

We can all admit that school has purposes in addition to preparing students for the workplace. No one believes this more strongly than us. On the other hand, it is true that most of us hope that what happens at school prepares our students for a successful life beyond school. The workplace is to some extent an indicator—but not the only one—of life success. The positive thing about the matter is this, that the classroom *is* a workplace. In other words, the future is now, it is already happening. So we can focus on the here and now with our students, which is more powerful than threatening them with skills they may need in some "distant" (to them) future.

It is also good news that emphasizing the skills addressed in this chapter does not mean deemphasizing the knowledge and skills of the academic curriculum. In fact, the social skills addressed here will enhance academic learning. Individual learning and individual effort will always be with us, have no fear. The best balance occurs when our students and teachers learn the joys of group *and* individual effort.

Learning Community Discussion Starters

1. In a general sense, how does school prepare students for careers? What skills, attitudes, and understandings best prepare students for career success?

2. Creativity and the ability to innovate are important career skills. In what ways does the typical school day encourage or discourage these skills?

Strategy 7

Authentic Applications

Education, in its larger sense, is one of the most inexhaustible of all topics.

— John Stuart Mill

During a ferry boat ride across Puget Sound near Seattle, we noticed art projects by primary age students prominently on display on the interior walls of the cabin. Passengers were looking at the children's work as though they were visitors to an art museum viewing great paintings. It was a delightful scene.

Purpose

Most schoolwork is academic, perhaps not in the sense that it is always so intellectually challenging, but academic in the sense that it is not put to use. This is unfortunate because it is in the *application* of knowledge, skills, and values that human beings find meaning. When ideas are not applied, they seem to start nowhere and go nowhere.

Imagine practicing for a play, one in which you are given a significant role, and then learning that the point of the whole experience was practice. There will be no production, no costumes, no makeup, no opening night, no combination of fear, excitement, and anticipation, no audience, no reviews, no parties held after the performance. Just practice.

Or, imagine a basketball team that practices daily: free throws, passing, rebounding, jump shots from the corner, defense, and the like. Imagine also that the coach tells you and your teammates from the start that there will be no games, no crowd, no enthusiasm, no fans screaming themselves hoarse, no league, no popcorn sold, just good old-fashioned practice. The whole idea seems preposterous. Why would we even consider it? The answer is that we would not.

Now let us focus on the classroom. Classrooms are places where great ideas are often introduced, ideas that have changed the world. This happens all the time when great literature, scientific discoveries, profound mathematical ideas, and great feats of exploration are taught to students. If this is so, then why is typical schoolwork not more exciting and engaging? One answer to this question is failure to apply ideas. The key is not so much the idea itself, many lessons and activities contain ideas that have unlimited potential. But potential is just that, something that could but has not yet occurred, as in potential energy before it is transformed into kinetic energy.

The purpose of the *Authentic Applications* strategy is to challenge you and your students to become involved in ways that transform the curriculum from one of potential energy to one of applied, functioning energy. And the key to doing this is to find as many outlets for student work as possible.

Procedure

Some of these outlets are obvious, just waiting for action. For example, when students do artwork such as painting and drawing, the usual routine is for their efforts to be sent home where some of it ends up decorating refrigerator doors. That is all right, but what about an intermediate step where the artwork done by the class is displayed at a senior citizens' home for a few days? This gives students an audience to think about and to share with, and it gives some retired folks a glimpse of school life. Who knows, perhaps some friendships will occur as a result.

Students in science classes often put together displays of scientific information, including diagrams, photographs, puzzles, models, experiments, posters. This is a perfect opportunity to contact the people at the local museum or library to see whether they would like to have the work put on display there. The chances are good that they will accept.

Philosopher and academic leader Robert Maynard Hutchins, who served for many years as the Chancellor of the University of Chicago, an elite academic school, once remarked that the reason students like extracurricular activities so much is because the curriculum is so stupid. Hutchins noted the excitement, pleasure, rewards, and genuine learning that accompany the experience of being in the band or orchestra, the debate team, athletic teams, yearbook, school newspaper, and clubs. He contrasted this with the sterile, unappealing atmosphere of most classroom academic environments. It doesn't have to be that way, but it will take you to change things.

Two words come to mind to describe the extracurricular activities: authentic and application. If you've ever worked on a school newspaper, you know that the authenticity derives from the fact that the newspaper is actually distributed. People read it. The deadlines are real, the grammar is applied, the written word finds an audience.

Of course not every lesson can be immediately applied. But the starting point is to decide right now that a great deal more of schoolwork *can* be authentically applied. This is why the best schools have school plays, science fairs, art fairs, concerts, games, something going all the time. These applications are the single best way to bring the public to the school and the school to the public. There is no better form of public relations for a school. The key to all this is to think in terms of projects. There should never be a time in your class when project learning is not emphasized. Projects are by definition authentic in that they are chosen by students, usually take team work, employ knowledge and skills as *tools* to be used, and result in some kind of display, performance, or other public outlet.

Outcomes

The reflective potential of *Authentic Applications* is tremendous. When students have displayed their work, been involved in a performance or competition, applied their abilities to an actual outcome, then there is indeed something to talk about, critique, analyze, and take pleasure in. Mark Twain once noted that in writing the difference between choosing the right word and the wrong word to express a thought is as great as the difference between lightning and a lightning bug. I wish to submit for your consideration the idea that the difference between schoolwork that is mainly practice and schoolwork that is applied in some authentic way is just as great. When authentic applications are made, then effort, pride in one's work, and even the critique itself take on a depth of meaning seldom found in typical schoolwork. "Practice sessions" even take on added significance, just as they do for an orchestra, the cast of a play, or an athletic team.

The theme of this book is teaching, learning, and assessment together to create reflective practice. Authentic applications of schoolwork help to create the necessary conditions. Knowing that your work will be displayed in some way changes the stage of preparation, so crucial in problem solving and creative effort. This foreknowledge enables a learner to think ahead to the event, lending a focus to the work. The stage in which the event itself takes place (e.g., science fair, athletic contest, play, concert) offers further opportunity for reflection, judgment, review, and analysis. And when the performance is over, this final stage represents a time to reflect, to think about meaning, truthfulness, beauty, effort, and to take the measure of what went right or wrong toward improvement in the future.

Differentiating *Authentic Applications*

 Student groups can tackle contemporary societal problems as an exploration of a literary theme or historical concept. For example, if students are reading Upton Sinclair's *The Jungle*, their awareness of the historical issues with workplace safety might give them a basis from which to investigate modern concerns and draw some comparisons or contrasts to the concerns presented to them. Students could then present their findings to a community council or other task force that is charged with oversight of workplace safety.

 Online investigations and reporting have become ever easier. Students might collaborate with a local media personality to shadow or participate in a social–action–research project. With the age of e-mail, students can directly contact those "in the mix" to forge connections and relationships that would allow students the opportunity to attain real-world experience and a method of reporting or sharing their work with an interested audience.

 Students could create a play or performance piece based upon the literature they are reading or the historical era they are studying. This could take the form of a historical narrative or something more creative. The key element is that students are afforded the chance to share their output in a meaningful way.

From the Classroom

Rachel Schwenn teaches high school history. She was looking for ways to help students forge meaningful connections between historical events and their day-to-day lives. This proved to be a repeating challenge as students had difficulty relating to these historical events. In talking with the kids, Rachel discovered that they were disengaging mainly because of how long ago they perceived the events to be, as well as the fact that the event didn't directly involve them or their family or friends. Rachel decided to use an *Authentic Applications* reflective assessment to help her students overcome their perceptions about historical events.

Rachel found a local nursing home facility that was within walking distance of her building. In a conversation with the director of the home, she found out that many of the residents were either veterans of World War II, or had been alive and living in the United States during that time. Rachel realized that this might be an opportunity for students to make deeper connections about their learning by having person-to-person interactions with people who experienced history first hand.

She talked with her students about the fact that they could get first-hand accounts of World War II America from these residents. Students enthusiastically supported an extra-credit project wherein they would interview various residents about their life during World War II and then create a photo memoir book. The book would capture both vintage and modern photos and interview segments from the residents. They would submit the book to an online publication processor and then gift a copy of the book to the nursing facility. The book project ended up being a success and many students actually purchased a copy for themselves. Here's what students said about their *Authentic Applications*:

I thought that talking with these people would be boring. But Mr. Jacobsen changed that! He actually served on a battleship in the Pacific, and he had a ton of stories to share. I had no idea that he would have such a vivid memory of his experiences. It was cool to hear about life on the ship and the battles he fought in. I don't think I could ever be that brave.

I talked with Ms. Eward, who was a housewife during World War II. I had no idea that everyday families did without so many things to support the war effort. I will never forget hearing her talk about having no pantyhose for two years, or how she had to go to the store on specific days and use coupons to buy food, even when she had enough money to pay for whatever she wanted! That was intense.

This project ended up being really awesome. I was nervous going to the nursing home the first time just because elderly people seem so grumpy when I encounter them. Surprisingly, the people that I talked to were really friendly and they seemed touched and excited that we were so interested in their experiences. The look on the faces of many of them when we made the book presentation is something I will always remember.

Improved Social Setting

We are supposed to be getting trained for society but are taught as if each one of us were going to live a life of contemplation in a solitary cell.

— Jean-Jacques Rousseau

Entire books have been written on the topics of working together, getting along, social skills, conflict resolution, and team building. A complete discussion of any of those matters is beyond the scope of this book. However, we ought not to minimize the role that social skills play in reflective thinking. They are a fundamental condition. Any teacher who has tried group work only to find that the groups never got to the task at hand simply because they were unable to function socially knows the accompanying sense of frustration. Any student who feels that he or she "did all the work" while other group members tagged along will be reluctant to want to repeat the experience. No wonder so many teachers retreat to the safety of an environment where students work alone seated at their desks in rows. To attempt group work in the absence of reasonably developed social skills is analogous to attempting mathematical problem solving with people who cannot do basic computation.

One of the best sources of help when it comes to developing social skills is Daniel Goleman's (1998) *Working with Emotional Intelligence*. Goleman points out something that experienced teachers know intuitively, and that is that young people's social skills are on the decline. He notes that "perhaps the most disturbing piece of data comes from a massive survey of parents and teachers that shows the present generation of children to be more emotionally troubled than the last. On average, children are growing more lonely and depressed, more angry and unruly, more nervous and prone to worry, more impulsive and aggressive" (p. 11).

Goleman lists five categories of requisite skills needed to work effectively with others in group settings. These skills represent the affective side, or as Goleman labels them, "emotional competence." They are as necessary, perhaps more so, than intellectual competence when it comes to group problem solving and shared experience, whether in school, the workplace, or in other settings. They are worth our examining at this point. We suggest that you make them topics of study and discussion with your professional learning community and with your students.

Personal Competence

Self-awareness is defined as "knowing one's internal states, preferences, resources, and intuitions" (Goleman, p. 26). Self-awareness includes *emotional awareness*, which is the ability to recognize one's emotions and their effects, *accurate self-assessment*, knowing one's strengths and limits, and *self-confidence*, a strong sense of one's self-worth and capabilities.

Self-regulation is the ability to manage "one's internal states, impulses, and resources" (Goleman, p. 26). Self-regulation includes *self-control*, keeping disruptive emotions and impulses in check, *trustworthiness*, maintaining standards of honesty and integrity, *conscientiousness*, taking personal responsibility, *adaptability*, or flexibility in handling change, and *innovation*, becoming comfortable with new ideas, approaches, and information.

Motivation is defined by Goleman as "emotional tendencies that guide or facilitate reaching goals" (p. 26). Motivation includes *achievement drive*, or striving to improve toward excellence, *commitment*, that is, aligning with group goals, *initiative*, or readiness to act, and *optimism*, that is, persistence in spite of obstacles and setbacks.

Social Competence

Empathy is defined as an "awareness of others' feelings, needs, and concerns" (Goleman, p. 27). Empathy includes *understanding others*, that is, showing interest in the concerns, feelings, and perspectives of others, *developing others*, or sensing others' needs and bolstering their abilities, and *service orientation*, anticipating, recognizing, and meeting others' needs.

Goleman defines *social skills* as "adeptness at inducing desirable responses in others" (p. 27). Social skills include *influence, communication, conflict management, leadership, cooperation, building bonds, and team capabilities*, all of which are aspects on integrating oneself meaningfully into the group as a supportive, caring, member who believes in the group's goals and wants to help fulfill them.

Those of you who are serious about developing social skills and what Goleman calls emotional intelligence need to read his book. You'll come away convinced that emotional intelligence (what we often think of as social skills) is probably more significant than the kinds of intelligence measured by traditional IQ tests.

Conclusion

Philosopher Jean-Jacques Rousseau wrote that "it is by doing good that we become good." We think his sage advice should be applied to the social context of classrooms. The social skills that we have outlined above represent desirable habits for young people to acquire. But how do they acquire them? The answer is simple: by *doing* them. The evidence shows us that students today are often deficient in social skills. The evidence also shows us that many students are deficient in their mathematics and reading skills. The remedy in either case is the same: practice with good coaching and opportunities to reflect on experience.

Learning Community Discussion Starters

1. What kinds of learning activities lend themselves to having students practice their social skills? Explain the advantages and disadvantages of designing and using these kinds of activities with students.

2. What would a homework assignment look like that emphasizes traits such as *self-regulation, understanding others,* or *social skills* for students who are working together on project assignments?

Strategy 8

Parents on Board

Show kindness to parents.

— The Qur'an

Purpose

It is widely known that parents are potentially the most important players in a child's education. We say *potentially* because although they do have the power to be of great influence, there are times when it seems that some of them are content to "let the schools take care of my child's learning." This is a mistake of tragic proportions. Philosopher Jurgen Habermas notes that one of the most debilitating problems of our time is the rise of "expert" cultures that take the place of home and neighborhood in handling tasks that home and neighborhood ought to handle. The best approach for teachers and administrators, of course, is for school to work together with the home. This is the most effective way to support a child's learning.

The *Parents on Board* strategy does what its name suggests, gets parents directly involved in their child's school work. It works best when it is used systematically and methodically. It is not designed to be an occasional approach to parent/child cooperation. It is an integrative strategy, that is, it is designed to integrate school life with home life.

Procedure

Here is how it works. Parents need to be asked in specific, concrete ways to offer their help. Generic pleas for them to be involved may reach a few, but most won't know what you want of them. One approach, suitable with younger children, is to use a form that parents sign and the children bring to you.

There are three levels of parent help that have promise. They range from minimally engaged to high levels of engagement. The first level is simply a concrete suggestion of something for them to do to facilitate their child's learning. It may be as simple as asking them to ensure that their child has a specific time and place to do homework. In this regard, the request is about the same as that made by the piano teacher who asks parents to be sure that the child practices playing the piano for a certain number of minutes per day. As simple as this idea is, it really does work. The establishment of routines for carrying out important tasks is a lesson to be learned early in life, and homework is a good place to start the process. As a professional, you may be surprised to learn that some parents have not thought of the idea of providing a specific place and time for their child to do his or her homework; but remember that parents need your advice and counsel more than you might know, especially the parents whose involvement levels are the lowest.

A second level of *Parents on Board* is that of helping a child to carry out his or her homework in ways that go beyond mere enforcement of time and place. For example, if you suggest that it is beneficial for parent and child to take a walk at least one evening a week, to watch and critique a television program together, to make plans to do a project of some kind (not necessarily related to school) around the home, then you have created the opportunity for parents and children to interact in meaningful ways. If one can believe the surveys that tell us that fathers, for example, spend less than five minutes per day interacting with their children, then you will have at the very least attempted to do something about that.

A third level of *Parents on Board* is that of inviting parents to take part in the curriculum itself. A common refrain from parents when their children reach intermediate and middle school years is that the mathematics is too difficult for them to understand. This is a perfect opportunity to start Family Math Night once or twice a month. Or Arts Night, Geography Night, Science Night, or Literature Night. You get the idea. By offering stimulating, engaging, easy-to-follow instruction to parents and their children together, you bring about a level of integration in the family that you might not have thought possible.

Some schools have benefited greatly by having everyone (teachers, students, staff) read the same book. It creates conversational opportunities that spill over from class to class. Why not take this brilliant idea one step further and invite parents on board? Who knows what will happen when you get the entire school community reading, talking, and writing together?

Outcomes

We know that not everyone thinks this approach will work for the reason that a certain number of parents do not care enough to become involved. We have two answers to this opposition, both of which are based on our own experience. The first is that we live in a less-than-perfect world. Of course not every parent is going to follow every suggestion you or I make. This should not surprise us. But you might be surprised by how many will respond to your sincere suggestions for their child's education. My second answer is that we simply cannot know to what extent parents will cooperate with us until we try to find out. And much of the high art of teaching is found in the trying! We can never guarantee an outcome for someone else, but we can guarantee that we will try our best to help others learn.

I have seen schools, from primary through secondary, that have filled gyms, libraries, and cafeterias to capacity with Family Night activities related to the curriculum. Invariably, the payoff is tremendous, ranging from good will to more focused parent participation. If you are serious about raising academic achievement and improving the social/moral fabric of school life, then you must get parents on board.

Differentiating *Parents on Board*

 Online forums are a fantastic way for parents to participate in the curricular discussions going on in their student's classroom. Parents can be given access to discussion threads or wikis that allow for them to contribute comments and/or post information that is relevant to the topic. This is especially effective if the students are studying an area in which a parent is an expert. For example, students may be studying aerial tactics used in World War II and some parents may work at Boeing, who manufactured many airplanes at that time period. Parents can contribute historical information, photos, and comments to a discussion or wiki. Teachers can also involve parents by having a participative blog area for parents to contribute input to curriculum, projects, and the like.

 Cooperative learning for this strategy would look a bit different from the others. Rather than peer cooperative groups, the cooperation would come in the form of having parents come into the classroom for conferences. The student and parent could partner up to create curricular, skill, or general learning goals for the student. Those goals could then be presented to the teacher, and the teacher contributes input and/or feedback on those goals.

 Special needs learners really benefit from having their parents be actively involved in their learning. Oftentimes this already happens via the IEP (Individualized Education Plan or Special Education Placement) process. However, teachers can take a cue from that process and create an IEP of sorts for all students. Parents can be a part of the creation of the student's individual learning plan and help be responsible for monitoring student progress on stated goals. This includes all students in a similar process as the special needs learners, which then gives those with disabilities a feeling that everyone is participating in that process rather than the student feeling he or she is being singled out from his or her peers.

This strategy can easily incorporate many elements of *Record Keeping* (Strategy 15) by having parents monitor and track student learning. Invite parents to participate in their child's learning experience in a very specific way, helping both students and parents attain ownership for participating.

From the Classroom

Karen Heidl started a literacy campaign with her seventh grade students and their parents. Her hope was to increase parent involvement in her classes as well as to increase the amount of reading done by all students in her class. She began an ongoing Literacy List project. This project involved students reading novels outside of class, discussing them with their parents or another adult, and then submitting notes of those discussions for a classwide discussion on a biweekly basis.

The rollout of the Literacy List program was threefold. First, she created an online discussion blog where students and parents would be able to record their discussion notes and impressions of the book as they were reading it. She then introduced the program to her students at the start of the school year. Finally, she kicked off the parent involvement portion of the program at the annual back-to-school parent night in late September.

Karen then had the students and parents begin reading the first novel. She would post discussion questions on the blog each week, which the student and parent could access either together or individually. Each week, Karen sent out an e-mail update to all parents and students, reminding them of where they should be in the reading of the book, as well as sharing the discussion questions for that week.

At the conclusion of each novel, parents were then invited into the classroom to participate in a class discussion about the novel. Karen had parents and students involved in a Socratic seminar-style discussion. Here are sample comments from a student and parent about their experience:

My mom had read our first novel a long time ago, so it was fun for her to re-read it and then to talk about what she thought about the book. I then put my own spin on it, and we had a great discussion. It was a lot of fun to talk with her and not be arguing about doing homework!

I have to admit that I've not done a lot of "fun" reading in my adult life. Being able to enjoy a novel and then talk about it with my child was really terrific. And then I thoroughly enjoyed the *online blog! Both posting comments and then reading the comments of others really got me thinking. I felt like a student all over again. What a great experience to share with my kiddo.*

Karen was so inspired by the success of the program that she will be continuing it for future classes. She is also sharing the concept with her colleagues, many of whom will be launching their own Literacy Lists next year.

The Nature of Knowledge

It is good to know what, useful to know how, and splendid to know why.

— Angela Rastrelli

The acquisition of knowledge is a central purpose of the school experience. Students come to school to learn, at least that is the hope. Parents send their children there for such a purpose. Teachers dream of higher achievement by their students. Academic knowledge, to be sure, is at the forefront, but knowledge of self and others is also considered an integral part of the process. So it is only proper that we spend some time reflecting on the nature of knowledge, and the questions, "What is knowledge?" and "How do we know what we know?" Beyond this lies the question, "What knowledge is of most worth?" Such questions ought to be in the forefront of any teacher's mind each time the teacher plans and teaches a lesson, and it is properly one to be explored by students as well.

Most dictionaries define knowledge as those facts, skills, abilities, and understandings of which one has some command. Memory is involved, but so is the ability to make applications. If we were to ask someone "what is two times four?" we would imagine that person "knows" $2 \times 4 = 8$ from memory, but we would also expect the person to be able to apply it to certain instances, for example, "four stacks of two dollars each makes eight dollars." If the person could not make such an application we would reasonably conclude he or she does not have knowledge of this. Such questions deal with the issue of *what* we know. *How* we know is yet another matter.

Basically there are three related ways in which we know what we know. None of them ever functions exclusively of the others simply because human beings are such complex creatures, but for purposes of analysis we separate them and consider each in turn. They are *knowledge received, knowledge discovered,* and *knowledge constructed* (Thut, 1957). Philosophically, how we know what we know must be considered apart from such a question as whether our knowledge is accurate. For example, one person might "know" that the world is flat, and another "know" that it is round. Each might possess such knowledge without possessing any means of proving his or her case. And the fact of the matter is that most of the knowledge we do have is subject to change, probably only approximately accurate, and, one hopes, open to new possibilities.

Knowledge Received

Let's begin with the most common way that you and I know what we know, that is, knowledge received. The basic idea is that someone knows something that you or I do not know, and they teach it to us by showing and telling. It is based on the premise of dependence by novice learners on experts. If, for example, you know that there are nine planets in our solar system, we can imagine that you read that in a science book or were told that by your teacher, that perhaps you acquired this knowledge by reading a textbook or seeing a film, or it is possible that you witnessed a model of the solar system at a museum. However, about the time you memorize that number, poor Pluto loses its status as a planet, and now we are down to eight.

The very attractive aspect of knowledge received also contains its potential danger, and that is its appearance of efficiency. You can dispense a great deal of information in one lecture. A textbook chapter can include sophisticated explanations of trigonometric functions or the prescribed order of numerical operations. A few pages in a science textbook can explain the entire process of photosynthesis or tell you how the universe was formed. No wonder we look to this way of knowing what we know as the basis of the school curriculum! But keep in mind the old saying, "If something seems too good to be true, it probably is."

So, although it is true that most of what you and I know is knowledge received, this is not necessarily a good thing. This is especially the case when knowledge received becomes the *heart* of the curriculum experience. Balance is the key, and to achieve balance, we must look to the other two ways of knowing as crucial teaching/learning partners of knowledge received.

Knowledge Discovered

We adapt new information to fit our experience, and each of us has different experiences even when we are doing the "same" activity. When Jean Piaget described teaching as the organizing of environments, this suggests to us that good teachers will establish settings where *discovery through experience* is at the core. This translates to learning centers, project learning, hands-on experience, teamwork, and other means appropriate to a given age group. The emphasis shifts from *teaching* in the traditional sense of presentation by the teacher to *learning* by students. This is a tremendous change, a complete shift in the center of gravity, and it should not be underestimated as a transformation of the environment. It is the pedagogical equivalent of crossing a frontier.

The curriculum may be basically the same on the surface. Students may, for example, be learning about the reasons for the seasons, the Pythagorean Theorem, or about citizenship. But instead of being *told* how these things work, they are encouraged to use discovery methods, in other words, to *find out for themselves.* To learn about the seasons might require gathering leaves, flowers, and seeds, as well as taking temperatures each day, measuring precipitation, plotting sun angles, recording the times of sunrises and sunsets, and keeping diaries and journals of the information. To learn about our political system, students can participate in student government and become involved in some way in the community in order to discover how the processes work. In both instances there would be a certain amount of explaining, informing, and the like, by the teacher, and reading as well as accessing other information sources, but the point is that such information is attached to the discovery process, and it is pursued for a reason. It is tempting for teachers to tell students how, why, when, and where. It seems more "efficient." However, when knowledge is discovered, ownership follows because the *responsibility* for learning rests with the learner.

Knowledge Constructed

There is yet another way in which we know what we know. This way of knowing is that of *knowledge as a human construction.* If knowledge received is represented by "being told," and knowledge discovered is represented by "finding out," then knowledge constructed is represented by "building and creating." The first two types of knowledge represent knowledge that is preexistent, that is, it is already in place, and the job of the learner is either to be informed by authority or to find out for him- or herself. Knowledge as a human construction is different. It tends to be original. It is *constructed* by the learner. It now exists whereas previously it did not. This is not to say that all knowledge constructed is completely original in every respect. However, if a student writes a poem, or builds a project, or paints a picture, then we can think of the effort as knowledge constructed. If a group writes and puts on a puppet show, or if a group performs an original dance number, if a class searches for the truth of conditions in their classroom, then we can think of such efforts as knowledge constructed.

Conclusion

Each way of knowing explained here is eminently worth pursuing in school settings. But balance must be kept in mind. What happens when the school experience and knowledge acquisition are based almost exclusively on being told either by teacher or text? This is all too often the case. The search for balance means honoring all three ways of knowing to the extent that all three are prominent. Students who discover, build, and create, but who seldom are required to read are impoverished. This is why the secret to good writing is that you have to read a lot of good writing. When a student expresses him- or herself in writing, this is an act of construction, but the balance is found when the coaching is there, when the reading is required, and when discovery about self and others is encouraged along the way. And whatever form knowledge takes in a school setting, the need for reflection and the continuous reconstruction of the experience is necessary.

When balance is achieved, when reflective thinking is taken seriously, when teachers act on the premise that the frontier from teaching to learning must be crossed, great things begin to happen. We witness the transformation of the classroom from a place of top-down authority and emphasis on information and skills, to a place of empowerment and the search for ideas and values.

Learning Community Discussion Starters

1. Why do you think school life is so much about knowledge received? What is the link between perceptions of efficiency and knowledge received?

2. What do you think are the connections between discovery, construction, and reflection?

Strategy 9
Search for Meaning

Learning, in the proper sense, is not learning things, but the meaning of things.

— John Dewey (1933/1998)

Purpose

A crucial difference in whether we learn something is the meaning or lack of meaning we attach to it. Meaning isn't the only variable in learning, but it is a powerful one. If something is meaningful, we respond, becoming animated and involved. Think of yourself playing in an "important" game or of being part of the crowd shouting yourself hoarse for the home team. Maintaining your attention is hardly a problem. If something seems less than meaningful, we find ourselves drifting off, becoming bored or uninterested. Have you ever walked by a classroom where students obviously were finding little meaning in whatever was going on? In their boredom they glance pathetically at you as though they were trying to make contact with humanity.

A young person learning to drive a car typically wants to learn because the activity has meaning. Few things in life are more important to a teenager than getting a driver's license. The same person who forgot to do his or her homework probably did so because it had low priority on some internal "meaningfulness" scale. Why do young people join gangs? Why do young people try out for athletic teams? Why do they participate in the school play? The choir? Why do children play with Legos or video games by the hour? The question for us is, "What can I do to help the kids I teach find meaning in their school experience?"

Meaning when applied to school experience, especially academic experience, is an elusive quality. The search for meaning in classroom experience represents one of the most purposeful but difficult quests for teachers and students. Few pursuits have greater metacognitive potential. Like most reflective strategies, the *Search for Meaning* must begin with oneself. What meaning does the subject matter you are teaching have for you? Is it merely required? Something you mastered long ago and now are bored with? Just a job to do? Or do you truly feel that what you are teaching is vitally needed by your students? You can't wait to share it with them? Do you believe that your own learning is extended through your teaching? No school subject has meaning apart from a desire to teach and learn it. It is the human connection that makes the difference. This is exactly why we need *you* in the classroom and not someone who sees teaching as just a job, one that provides indoor work with no heavy lifting.

Procedure

The *Search for Meaning* assessment strategy represents an attempt to reflect on the moral implications of the learning experience. Whether your students and you conduct this procedure as a written task for each individual, use a discussion group approach, or a combination of both, the questions to ask include the following:

♦ In what ways does this activity (e.g., assignment) have meaning for me personally?

♦ How specifically might others benefit (or not) from the experience?

♦ Does this activity make my classmates and me better for having done it? In what ways?

♦ Is this the best use of our time?

♦ Is this experience enjoyable and fulfilling in other ways?

♦ Are all of us, not just some of us, involved?

These questions represent a place to start a process of reflection and a search for meaning. We encourage you and your students to add others that address the specific issues and goals you are trying to achieve. To the extent that you and your students are willing to write about and/or discuss meaning in learning, a classroom becomes a more truthful, open, and humane place.

Outcomes

Don't expect too much from your students at the outset. They may never have been asked to think, write, and talk about such questions. This is a time for patience on your part. It may not have occurred to them that they should be raising issues of morality, importance, and meaning about their school work. Improvement will come with time. As your students begin to realize that your own search for meaning in learning is genuine and that you deeply desire that for them, they will respond—just give them time.

Two additional outcomes of the *Search for Meaning* strategy are worth mentioning. First, this is a practical strategy. It is eminently practical to share and know to what extent you and your students find the work you do to be useful and meaningful. Why would you *not* want to know that? Places of voluntary association know about such practical matters on the basis of whether people show up, and whether they encourage their friends to get involved. But school is compulsory, thus we must look for more subtle practical manifestations. This is the place of conversation, of writing, and other means of signaling level of commitment.

The second outcome is one of efficacy or empowerment. We tend to appreciate it when people genuinely want to know how we feel, what we think, and how meaningful we find something. It represents an invitation. It gives us a voice in matters. It implies that needed changes will be made. Such empowerment brings with it a sense of responsibility. Genuineness is a two-way street. Just as the invitation to speak up, to lead, to offer suggestions is sincere, so must the responsibility to share one's best thoughts and ideas be sincere. We talk a great deal about leadership skills, and here is an opportunity for students to develop them.

Differentiating *Search for Meaning*

You may initially think that such a personal activity would not lend itself to any kind of cooperative learning strategy, but this activity naturally lends itself to an introspective small-group discussion in the classroom setting. It is the perfect way to tackle difficult topics in a supportive environment. A great way to share the more personal ideas of students that are created via this activity is to have students type up their comments but leave their names off the paper. Student ID numbers or another coding system could be implemented so the teacher can track who wrote which statement. Have students meet in pairs or small groups of no more than four students. Student statements can be shuffled up by the teacher, and then a handful distributed to each group of students. The discussion can center on shared meaning, areas of differentiation, concerns, or conclusions that the group infers from the statements. If the topic is particularly sensitive, the teacher can provide groups with guiding questions to facilitate the discussion. Groups could then redistribute the statements in a *Jigsaw* (Strategy 5)-like fashion and/or report on what they uncovered via their discussion.

Oftentimes introspective comments are found in the most amazing places. A great way to share the insights of students while protecting anonymity would be to create a "music video" to show what groups learned about their peers (or the content, or the class climate) to the full class. This video could either be created by the teacher as a way to share comments or it could be created by students as a way for them to assimilate information and condense the most relevant aspects of what their peers wrote. For a student-created video, create student groups and share copies of *Search for Meaning* statements (this could be done anonymously as outlined above). Student groups would then use movie-making or presentation slide software to present their project. They could pick a theme song or music that encapsulates the topic or starter question that would play in the background. Students could create slides with quotes from the *Search for Meaning* statements and photos or art that tie in to the topic at hand. The music videos could be shared at the start of class for the next few days or there could be a viewing party—complete with popcorn—at the conclusion of the project.

 Delving into emotions and making connections can be difficult for many special needs students, especially for those who have a disorder such as autism or Asperger's syndrome. Providing more concrete cueing may be a way to help those students tap into their emotional responses to create some level of context or meaning. Also, allowing students to dialogue rather than write might be helpful. Pairing these students with a peer and giving them some privacy might allow them to talk through ideas and find that deeper meaning.

 A teacher can take this activity to an entirely different level simply by the way the opening questions are crafted or by setting some parameters for the student responses. The teacher could require that the student make a comparison with another learning experience, or with a particular literary piece, or with a current or historical event. Not only does the student reflect on their particular experience, they also reflect on how they have become connected to the information they are learning in class. An essential part of having students produce higher level *Search for Meaning* statements is that students be given time to revisit their thoughts and improve upon them. An interesting way to do this would be to have a *Search for Meaning* section in their class notebook so that students maintain a record of their thoughts about their learning throughout the year. As the year progresses, students would be asked to forge greater connections to prior learning experiences and then be asked to discuss how they have grown as a learner (and what evidence they have to support that).

From the Classroom

Dan Freeborn, a high school teacher, came up with the "Walden Project" assignment. Dan tells the story of how his class was studying the writing of Henry David Thoreau, who wrote that, "most men live lives of quiet desperation" because they don't really follow their dream. So, Dan asked his class to think about, as individuals, what would you *really like to learn about?*

As Dan tells it, the students weren't prepared for such a question from a teacher. They didn't know what to say. He told them to let it percolate for a few days. Gradually, the students started coming forward with their ideas. One girl said she didn't know why, but she always wanted to learn Russian. A boy said he would like to learn to play the guitar but he couldn't afford to buy one. In time, every student had a project of his or her choice. What Dan "proved" was that every student has a dream. Today, the girl is a Russian major at university. Dan found a used guitar he gave to the boy and taught him to play.

The Walden Project was an exciting experience for students and teachers alike. Other teachers who tried this approach chose their own project, for example, learning how to play chess. Once the project got underway, teachers discovered that several students also decided they wanted to learn the same thing as the teacher. When this happens, the teacher takes on the roles of learner and mentor simultaneously! The students become especially interested in finding out what the teachers decided to learn during the project, furthering the personal connection between students and teacher. Here are some comments by teachers about their experience with trying out the "Search for Meaning" approach in the way of the Walden Project.

I really got to know the kids better as a result of doing this project.

Discipline was hardly an issue because the students were learning what they wanted to learn.

At first managing things was hard, but once everyone got going, the class ran on autopilot.

The toughest thing was helping the kids who couldn't decide what they wanted to learn. But that got me closer to them as we talked about choosing a topic. In the end, they all got on board.

The most common "complaint" was "please can we have more time to work on our projects?" I love those kinds of complaints at school!

I've learned the fine art of scrounging as a result of this. It's amazing the resources that are out there.

I like to think we've set some dreams in motion.

Ways to Learn

Mind is an extension of the hands and tools that you use and of the jobs to which you apply them.

— Jerome Bruner, *The Culture of Education*

Jerome Bruner

Psychologist Jerome Bruner (1966) described three learning modes that, taken together, bring balance to the curriculum and variety to the experiences through which teachers and students explore ideas, solve problems, and reflect on meaning. Bruner called these three learning modes enactive, iconic, and symbolic.

♦ *Enactive learning* is basically learning by doing. It is represented by hands-on learning, direct engagement, construction, and the like. It is sometimes called sensory learning because it engages the five senses directly. Another name for this type of learning is experiential learning.

♦ *Symbolic learning* is well known and widely practiced, perhaps too much so. Symbolic learning is represented primarily by words and numbers, in other words, text in the traditional sense. Reading, writing, and mathematics, when they are text-driven, are examples of symbolic learning.

♦ *Iconic learning* is found somewhere between enactive and symbolic forms. As the term *icon* implies, pictorial or graphic representation is the key. Pictures, graphs, maps, film, video, CD-ROM, drawings, and the like, are the ways in which iconic representation is expressed. Thus iconic learning is not as abstract as symbolic learning, but it is not as experiential as enactive learning.

Bruner's argument is that all three are necessary. The school experience should be one in which appropriate balance is found. All too often, the school day is dominated by symbolic learning, while the other two modes play a greatly diminished role. Symbolic learning, in the form of reading, writing, and listening to teacher talk, is useful to be sure, but symbolic representation depends for much of its power on the nature of the experience a learner brings to it. As many an enlightened educator has warned us, it is not at all helpful to assume experience on the part of children and adolescents because it is so often lacking in their young lives. An unpredicted but very real outcome of the standards movement is a retreat by teachers to a narrow perimeter of "basic skills" teaching using symbolic learning forms, thus unwittingly denying students the very hands-on, active experiences they so desperately need.

Consequently, if students are taught that the circumference of a circle is found by multiplying pi (3.14) times the diameter, very little true understanding takes place unless the teaching and learning are enriched through such experiences as finding circles in the environment (they are everywhere) and actually testing the formula, and other applied encounters. On the one hand, imagine the intellectual and social poverty of students who are limited to reading about saving the environment compared to those students whose teacher organizes an environmental study in which students take water and air samples, do fish and bird counts, make their own maps of the area under study, and otherwise become actively engaged in the investigation. On the other hand, imagine the intellectual poverty of actually trying to restore the environment without reading about the issues. So the argument is for balance, true balance.

Basic skills subjects such as reading and mathematics, when done in connection with investigations, projects, and hands-on learning, take on added meaning because those skills become necessary to the problem-solving process. They serve as tools or instruments that are absolutely needed in the same sense that garden tools are needed in a gardening project.

The key to balance is ensuring that all students learn through all three modes (see The Ecology of Learning below). Each mode supports the others in ways that bring about an ecology of learning that is truly symbiotic. Thus, when a unit is in the planning stages, and teachers and students are figuring the ways in which they will approach issues, it is useful to think of ways to balance activities so that equal representation occurs.

The Ecology of Learning

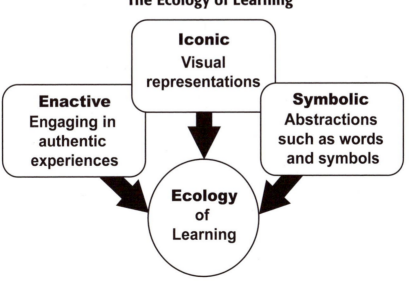

Multiple Intelligences Theory

 Howard Gardner's work in the field of multiple intelligences theory is also an instructive way to think about how people learn. Gardner concludes, as many others have, that the traditional view of intelligence is too restrictive, too limiting. His research in a variety of contexts led him to challenge the prevailing wisdom of intelligence as mainly paper and pencil, abstract abilities, and the like. Out of his investigations came the idea that intelligence manifests itself in distinctly different ways, including such forms of intelligence as verbal–linguistic, mathematical, spatial, musical, intra- and interpersonal, kinesthetic, and naturalist. Although Gardner's theory has been criticized for a lack of empirical evidence, the point remains that students need a variety of ways of challenging them to learn and to show their abilities to learn.

Conclusion

Both Bruner and Gardner argue for some kind of reasonable balance in the learning equation. We have known for some time that traditional paper-and-pencil approaches to learning, while valuable, are simply too restrictive.

Bruner reminds us that words and symbols represent only one of three major roads of access for the learner. The other two—hands-on activity and iconic representation of ideas—need to be given parity as you and your students plan and carry out learning experiences.

Learning Community Discussion Starters

1. Why do you think schools seem to focus so prominently on symbolic forms of learning?

2. How would classrooms be different if teachers simply acted on the principle of balance regarding Bruner's three modes of learning?

I Can Teach

Glady wolde he lerne and gladly teche.
— Geoffrey Chaucer, *The Canterbury Tales* (1387)

By leaning you will teach; by teaching you will understand.
— Latin proverb

Purpose

A century ago, John Dewey (1897) wrote that there will be real progress in education when teachers become learners and learners become teachers. Teaching as learning works particularly well when the teacher is also an enthusiastic learner, and learning as teaching works well when students are given opportunities to become teachers. In any real sense, teaching and learning are two sides of the same coin.

Teaching functions best when a symbiotic relationship develops between the desire to learn and the desire to share what one has learned. Invariably, the best teachers are those who are eager to learn their subject matter and who want more than anything to share their enthusiasm for learning with the young. When knowing, sharing, and caring come together people will learn. You can't hold them back.

Procedure

The *I Can Teach* strategy puts students into the dual role of learner and teacher. It challenges them to learn something not merely to acquire knowledge or to pass a test, but to learn something well enough to be helpful to others. There is a deeply imbedded, empowering moral purpose here, and that is that knowledge worth gaining, is also worth sharing with others.

The payback is wonderful. The learner who becomes a teacher will take his or her own understanding to deeper levels while experiencing the joy of seeing someone else begin to understand. This is basically the model that was used in Mexico many years ago to increase literacy throughout the country. The project was called "each one teach one." The idea was that each person who was *taught* to read taught someone else to read. It was enormously successful, and the literacy rate soared.

Here is how the *I Can Teach* strategy proceeds. At the conclusion of a lesson or series of lessons around a common theme, you challenge your students to think about and write down, diagram, or map a way that they could teach what they just learned to someone else. This is obviously effective with "older" students who teach something to "younger" students, for example, eleventh graders teaching an idea to ninth graders. Of course, the technique can also be applied at peer levels or by having students teach something they learned to their parents. Let us look at each of these three applications in more detail.

Students who are challenged to teach something they have learned to younger learners must take several things into account. First, comes the abiding question, "How well do I know this skill, idea, or content?" The answer must be something like, "I know this at a deeper level than just that of memory or passing exam questions that demand only recognition or recall."

If, for example, the challenge is teach a simple origami art activity learned at school, the students who will teach it at home need to know two things: *how to do it* and *how to teach it*. Psychologist Jerome Bruner wrote many years ago that it is possible to teach anything to anyone if it is done in an intellectually honest way. If this is so, what kinds of accommodations would be necessary in order for students who have learned this at school to teach it at home, perhaps to a younger sibling? What preparations would be necessary if a class of older students were to teach origami art to a class of younger learners? Obviously, the "teacher" would need to use concrete materials or something oriented toward a "hands-on" approach. Teaching reinforces learning. French essayist Joseph Joubert wrote that, "to teach is to learn twice over." How true.

Applied at a peer level, the *I Can Teach* strategy is useful as a means of bringing certain students up to speed on an idea or skill. The coverage mentality so prevalent in our schools compels teachers to keep moving on to the next lesson in order to complete the curriculum. It is an unfortunate mentality and one that is unendorsable by thoughtful people, but it is nevertheless a reality. So, *I Can Teach* affords a perfect opportunity for those who do understand an idea or skill to teach it to their classmates who do not. Everyone benefits.

Another application of *I Can Teach* is for, say, ninth graders to teach seventh graders. This makes for a splendid opportunity for creating a greater sense of community at school. Older students helping younger students represents a wise use of a resource seldom tapped. The social benefits are real as well. And why not have the younger students share something important they have learned with older kids? When these kinds of interactions take place in a school, the social/moral fabric begins to change. People get to know each other. Community happens.

I Can Teach is a perfect homework assignment in which students are asked to teach something they have learned in your class to their parents or brothers and sisters. This serves several purposes.

- First, it is a communications tool between school and home. Parents get a chance to find out experientially what their child is being taught at school. Awareness is created; linkages are formed.

- Second, the student is given another opportunity to revisit the material, this time from the perspective of explainer. This is reinforcement of something important at its best. One of your long-range goals ought to be to create conditions for parents and children to talk to each other. This gives them a reason to do so and a vehicle for doing it.

- And third, when students report back on the success of their venture at home, the material is visited for yet a third time. What if students had trouble teaching the idea? This tells you something you need to hear. Remember that anything worth learning is worth learning well.

We recommend a procedure whereby you give students an opportunity to put on paper their ideas for teaching the activity; younger students will need to do this orally. Once students have written down or diagrammed their ideas, they should form triads (groups of three) that meet for fifteen minutes or so to share insights, ideas, methods, materials, and whatever else might be needed to teach the content effectively. To the extent that you think it is helpful, you can take an active part in making suggestions, especially the first few times you use this strategy.

It is crucial to have followup discussions that focus on how well things went. This is a way of reflecting back on the experience in order to make sure that improvement occurs over time. By the time the year ends, you will have sown a whole new crop of teachers.

Outcomes

I Can Teach is designed to empower students with the thought that knowledge is something you use, not just something you keep in the storehouse of the mind until examination time. This strategy asks students to cross a threshold from learning as something only for oneself to learning as something you pass along to others. Learning is transformed from acquisition to performance. You know the pleasure of helping people learn. It is time to share that pleasure with your students. Use it or lose it.

Differentiating *I Can Teach*

This strategy inherently relies on students collaborating with each other. There are many ways of doing this, as mentioned in the *Outcomes* and *Procedures* sections of this strategy. Another interesting way to go about this is for the teacher to pair up with a colleague and have each class learn a different topic concept. Then have students in each class diagram a way to present what they just learned to their peers in the other classroom. After preparing and practicing, each group would present its lesson to the other class, and vice versa.

Online "live" classrooms provide a wonderful way for students to learn from one another. Your class could set up a peer-tutoring wiki or blogosphere where students take turns being the expert that tutors or teaches their peers. This could also be employed to help absent students keep up with missed work.

Students can be challenged to not just reteach what they just learned, but to take their lesson to the next step by finding and researching primary source documents, investigating biographies of authors or historical figures, or enriching what they learned with cultural elements from the time period of the literary piece or historical era. In essence, they are deepening their connections and providing a richer lesson than what was given to them initially.

This strategy is a natural for use with *Jigsaw* (Strategy 5). Divide the students into equally sized groups. Have each group of students receive instruction or experience content in a specific area that is unique to that particular group. After the instructional segment is concluded, each person in that unique group is now a "subject expert" on that topic. They then partner with the other subject experts from other groups, and each student takes turns teaching their segment of the content.

From the Classroom

Pam Johnson is a high school English teacher and is also the advisor for the school's National Honor Society program. The students in the Honor Society were discussing ideas for an ongoing philanthropy project that would be fun and also benefit schools in some way. After many meetings with several ideas brought up and rejected, Pam worked with students to come up with a great project idea: students in the club would visit students in the local middle schools each week at the same appointed time to work with them on academic skills. Some students elected to take on an intensive reading program where they would teach the middle school students reading strategies, while other students decided to teach a math skills session with students at those middle schools.

The teachers at the middle schools were so excited about the program that they made themselves available to help facilitate the study sessions. The teachers quickly realized that their help was unnecessary, because the students were very invested in making the program work. The Honor Society students were amazingly well prepared and had done a lot of preparatory work to ensure their lessons would be successful. Once the middle school teachers saw the level of dedication and preparation of the tutors, they began actively promoting the program and recruiting students to attend the sessions.

This year, the program was so popular that additional student support from the high school was necessary. Today, every Honor Society member has a mini-group of middle school students whom they teach reading or math concepts weekly. Middle school teachers are reporting that students involved in receiving tutoring are demonstrating regular gains in their academic achievement. Furthermore, the teachers of the students who are doing the tutoring report that those students are grasping content more quickly and thoroughly than they did prior to becoming tutors.

Equally as important as the academic benefits, the relationships forged between the tutors and their middle school students has paid off in another way. Friendships and shared understanding are happening across grade levels in a way that had not happened before. According to Pam, the students receiving tutoring seem to have a smoother transition to the high school setting as they already know students in the building. In this way, *I Can Teach* not only has academic benefits, it also has social/moral benefits that extend beyond the classroom setting.

The Curriculum and Principles of Learning

For the things we have to learn before we can do them, we learn by doing them.

— Aristotle

Take a moment to reflect on Aristotle's insight. What does he mean? What is he saying about a principle of learning? How would his comment relate to learning to ride a bicycle? How would it relate to learning to read?

A reflective activity for you to take seriously is that of reviewing certain principles of learning in order to determine to what extent you actually are carrying them out on a daily basis. A simple way to do this is to make a checklist of them and quickly review them at the beginning or end of the day. An even better way is to discuss them regularly with fellow teachers and members of your team or professional learning community.

With this brief introduction, let us examine the principles themselves with the hope in mind that they will become an integral part of your thinking, feeling, and doing toward the goal of a reflective classroom.

♦ Teaching is a means, learning is an end.

It is easy to forget in the busy world of lesson plans, instruction, exams, and report cards that *learning* is the purpose of school. We often ask ourselves the question, "What is good teaching?" The answer to the question is good teaching is that which results in good learning. This means that your teaching should be strategic, that is, oriented toward the two goals or larger outcomes that we encountered earlier: raising achievement and improving the social/moral fabric (see Strategy 5: *Jigsaw*). This allows you to change tactics to fit the situation at hand without losing sight of the strategic goal.

♦ Learning takes practice.

It is well documented that we get better at those things we practice. This is particularly true when our practice is accompanied by good coaching. We read recently about a major league third baseman who regularly fields 400 ground balls a day in practice. No wonder he makes difficult plays look like routine plays! Practice is the crucial difference between someone who aspires to be truly good at something and someone who is willing to settle for mediocrity.

Those who aspire to excellence are disciplined, that is, they are willing to put in hours of practice (it could be writing, reading, friendship, golf, sewing, geography, or something else), and they are open to expert help in the form of encouragement and criticism. We talk about children and adolescents becoming good readers, but if we are serious about this worthy goal, then we are going to have to expect far more reading by them than is generally required. When we notice that a student is a good writer, we invariably discover that this person reads a lot.

♦ The rich get richer, and the poor get poorer.

Schema theory suggests that our ability to comprehend something is typically more a matter of prior knowledge than of innate ability. Thus the earlier one becomes a habitual reader the better. The earlier one begins to grasp number concepts, the more one is able to learn them at advanced levels. But it is crucial to bear in mind that we are never too old to learn. Good habits can and should be developed throughout a lifetime. So, whatever the age level of students you teach, think of them as learners who need to be gently nudged toward habits of reading, writing, reflecting, and responsibility.

Studies of motivation to learn academic subjects show that the single largest factor is prior knowledge of subject matter. How many otherwise talented students are there who have given up on mathematics by middle school, who could have been perfectly capable of learning geometry, trigonometry, physics? They choose not to learn because they lack basic knowledge, not because they lack ability. Knowledge builds on knowledge; it is self-sustaining and self-generating. The more you know, the more you want to know.

♦ A little chaos is a good thing.

In their excellent book, *Models of Teaching,* Joyce et al. (2008) use the terms *syntax* and *syntactic complexity* with reference to the structure of classroom environments. These terms are obviously borrowed as metaphor from grammar, but they are very useful as ways to think about the everyday activities and routines of your classroom. Syntax is an element of structure, whether we are talking about the structure of a sentence or the structure of an academic/social situation. Ask yourself, "How simple or how elaborate is the syntax of my classroom?" Simple syntax is achieved by placing students in rows, each at his or her own desk, working essentially alone. Syntactic complexity is achieved through freedom of thought, speech, and movement. It takes the form of projects, cooperative learning, conversation, shared reflection, and other activities that bring people together.

♦ Learning at its best is a collaborative endeavor.

The myth of the lone achiever, whether in scientific research, Western films, or school work, dies hard. It is still not uncommon to hear teachers say, "Please keep your eyes on your own work and your hands to yourself." The implication of such a statement is that each person should develop his or her own thoughts and keep them *intellectually, socially, morally,* and *physically* sequestered. Unfortunately, this model inhibits development of the whole person. We desperately need more classrooms where students think and plan together, where projects are valued, where positive interaction is encouraged, and where the opportunities to reflect on meaning are real. Check any current article on skills needed in the workplaces of the future, and you'll see an emphasis on collaborative skills, team building, an ability to discuss ideas without becoming defensive, and the desire to work with others to get things done.

♦ Manners are close to morality.

A typical school classroom is one of the more crowded environments you'll ever find. Too many people, not enough space—this is the norm, not the exception. No wonder so many teachers require their students to sit quietly at desks in rows. It is, after all, one means of crowd control. Earlier we discussed the need for a certain amount of chaos, and now we encounter its corollary. A reasonably chaotic environment is good because it is necessary for the conditions whereby more complex interactions can take place. But such an environment must be civil. A classroom, of all places, must be a place where people are treated with and treat others with dignity, respect, honor, and politeness. Without such conditions firmly in place, a classroom begins to degrade, academically and morally.

A home typically has far fewer people and far more space than a school classroom. And it has the benefit of family ties, affections, and of being *private* space. A classroom, on the other hand, is *public* space where people congregate to learn about the world, life, each other. Public space demands certain agreed upon and enforced rules and norms of behavior in order to function well. Words like "please" and "thank you" go a long way toward creating civility. When a classroom becomes a place of intellectual challenge *and* social civility, it is transformed into something memorable.

Learning Outcomes

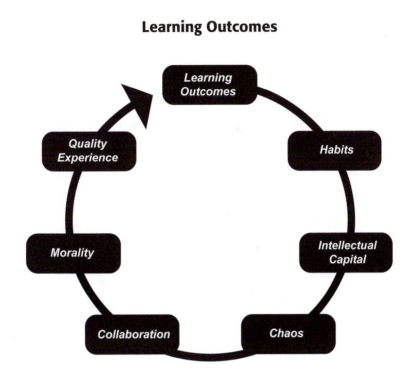

Conclusion

A productive classroom environment is an active one to be sure. Students are busy working together, and a teacher's job is to make sure the workplace is friendly with an underlying structure of harmony and discipline. To maintain a largely positive atmosphere, you may wish to invoke the "two for one" rule so often used in successful work environments. This rule states that for every negative comment a person offers, he or she must accompany it by at least two positive comments.

Opportunity for reflection means opportunity to raise fundamental questions. How meaningful is this activity? Are we learning things that are truly valuable? How do the things we are doing help us to be better citizens? Are we really giving our best effort? What can we do to make sure that every person is involved in some purposeful way? Are we doing things that really interest us? How honest are we being about our work? The list of questions can go on. These will do for starters if you decide that you want a challenging, reflective place for you and your students to teach and learn.

Learning Community Discussion Starters

1. It is said that a good parent understands the balance between nurture and discipline. In what sense is this also true of a good teacher?

2. What are the defining characteristics of classroom *chaos* with an underlying structure that encourages learning and *chaos* that is simply the product of poor classroom management?

Strategy 11
Write It Down

All you have to do is write one true sentence. Write down the truest sentence you know."

— Ernest Hemingway's advice to anyone star-
ing a blank piece of paper

Purpose

The witty Irish comedian Hal Roach would often pause reflectively and dramatically following one of his better jokes, giving the audience ample time to roar with laughter. When the howling had finally subsided, he'd draw yet another laugh by saying, "write it down," the idea being that if you do you're sure to remember it, and you just might want to tell the joke to your friends.

Philosopher Mortimer Adler said he always kept a small notepad in his pocket, and when he was introduced to someone, he would take out the notepad and write down the person's name. He said it does wonders for the memory. The habit of taking notes in class takes practice, and such practice leads to better learning. It doesn't take a great deal of skill; merely establishing a habit of writing down thoughts that seem important during a lesson. Try this experiment with your class. Make some notes about the important ideas, skills, and knowledge in a lesson. Then teach the lesson, asking your students to take notes during it. Afterward, hold a reflective session with the class in which you compare your notes for the lesson with the notes they have taken. This is a wonderful opportunity to "gently" teach note-taking skills.

We have friends who are enthusiastic journal keepers. They write in their journals every day. As a result, they visit important events at least four times: (1) the event itself; (2) the recording of the event; (3) the pleasure of reading about the event days, months, or years later; and (4) the clearer meaning and understanding of events in perspective. The difference in levels of awareness between the diarist and those who keep no written record of their lives is profound.

Procedure

Following are several key questions for you and your students to pose in order to improve the quality of the journal keeping experience:

♦ How selective and strategic are my journal entries?

To paraphrase the old Bob Seeger song, *Against the Wind*, "what to leave in, what to leave out." To what extent do the entries reflect on the things we are studying? To what extent am I able to connect the school experience with my life experience in general? Unless connections are made, students will never achieve what philosopher Alfred North Whitehead called "the seamless whole" in learning.

♦ What are the sources of my thoughts and entries?

It has been noted that the two main avenues of human growth and development are the ideas we encounter and the people we get close to. This is a good place to start—with ideas and relationships. Other things tend to fall into place in their wake. Students need to be encouraged to enter ideas from the books they read, the material they study, the discussions in which they are involved. Because keeping a journal represents writing as learning, it is useful to keep in mind Charles Osgood's observation that a person's writing is only as good as the books they read. But there is also an affective side to the matter, and this is the function of relationships with others. A good journal is a blend of thoughts *and* feelings.

♦ What insights to personal growth am I gaining?

The important terms here are *insights* and *personal.* Am I becoming more reflective? How? In what ways? Am I improving my character, becoming a better person? Am I more interested in learning? Do I seek knowledge beyond the minimal school requirements? Am I in closer touch with my feelings? Am I growing in the area of becoming more involved with others? To what extent am I reaching out to others?

♦ What provisions are made for feedback?

Your feedback should be based on the premise that you have actually read the journals, and beyond that your remarks should reflect the first three questions posed in this procedure (described in this section). You need to constructively criticize and support your students' efforts to explore ideas, to go to the best available sources, to include appropriate content, and to show some measure of insight in their writing.

Outcomes

Note taking and journal keeping expand the thought processes and provide means of personal exploration and reflection. Note taking makes a person an active listener who will recall more than the person who doesn't do it. A journal's very privacy, intimacy, and personal content make it a powerful avenue for learning. Because each individual decides what he or she will enter in the journal, the experience is customized, allowing for and inviting different perspectives, different senses of what really matters, and a unique opportunity for each person to express those things that have the greatest individual relevance and meaning. So, *write it down!*

Differentiating *Write It Down*

Students can collaborate on journaling by peer editing one another's work on a regular basis. Student collaboration can also take place in form of a dialogue, where students share their thoughts with peers regarding content, learning processes, or pathways to mastering information or skills.

Students can maintain their journal in a blog format online. This allows students to access their current and past writing easily. Blogs can be updated, changed, edited, or just have a new entry added to the growing list. Most blog sites can be controlled to be semipublic or private so as to allow only the authoring student and teacher to see the entries or to allow only a predetermined group of students to view and/or contribute feedback or responses.

A journal is an excellent way for struggling learners to attain and master organizational skills that will benefit them in their current learning and long-term learning. By recording their daily thought processes or assignments in one key location, students have a ready-made review guide for assessments or research purposes. These journals can be maintained for an entire unit of study or by a calendar timeline.

Journals can be used to multitask. By dividing up sections or daily pages, students can track homework, daily warmups, and daily activities; even their individual work that was completed during class or at home. By providing a table of contents or other tracking device (see *Strategy 15: Record Keeping*) journals become an effective tool for grading. Students place their materials in the order outlined in their table of contents and the teacher can follow the order to grade the assignments.

Journaling can be taken in a variety of directions. Having students focus on solid writing practices in their journaling is way for students to get repetition on expository, narrative, or reflective writing styles. Students could be asked to identify elements of essays in their writing by diagramming or underlining. Journals can also be used to have students "step into someone else's shoes," be it an author, a main character, or a historical figure from their learning. By doing this students are forced to consider other perspectives and viewpoints, as well as hone their writing from first person and/or third person perspectives.

Combine *Write It Down* with *Search for Meaning* (Strategy 9), *Week in Review* (Strategy 3), or *Key Idea Identification* (Strategy 6) by having students focus their journal writing on a specific prompt or topic area. This can be enhanced by having students *Jigsaw* (Strategy 5) or *Think Aloud* (Strategy 2) to peer edit, review, or provide feedback to their peers about their writing.

From the Classroom

Doug Marcoux wanted to assign a semester-long project to his students that would encapsulate their learning about the history of the twentieth century, but he feared that assigning such a large, long-term assignment might not be a successful undertaking. After talking about the project with colleagues, he settled upon incorporating a *Write it Down* element to the project. Although there would be a final product as well as documentation of process (edits and revisions, etc.), Doug included a journal segment that would be reviewed by the teacher on a weekly basis.

Students would write in their journals daily, recording their progress on the assignment, identifying next steps, and reflecting on their thoughts about how it was all going. Initially, Doug thought this would be a big gamble, and he worried that students wouldn't make use of the journal in a productive and efficacious way. He was pleasantly surprised to see that students not only kept their journals updated, but that their writing demonstrated true reflection of their work and thoughts. Here are some sample entries:

> Today I finally finished the technology element for the project. This had been something that was keeping me up at night so it felt great to get it done! Now I need to really focus on solidifying my research and putting the citations into my written paper. This project seemed almost un-do-able when Mr. Marcoux first assigned it, but since we do a little bit each week, it's actually kind of fun.

I think I am a bit behind today and that is making me feel a little stressed. I realize by not really focusing right off the bat I lost some valuable research time, and now it looks like I will need to make a trip to the local library to get the next steps completed. Not going to make that mistake again... hope to catch up this weekend and then try to begin getting ahead. So far I like the project and I am hoping I can get some inspiration to take it to the next level.

I'm wondering how to accomplish so many elements even though we have so much time! I can see that Mr. Marcoux hopes the journal will organize us. It's a struggle, but when I think about figuring out what needs to happen next it does help me break down the assignment. I wonder if I tried that with my science project if I would feel better about doing it?

Beyond the pleasant surprise of finding that the journals contained meaningful information, Doug found that the students who were the most diligent in maintaining their journals also completed the final projects at a higher level. Perhaps even better, when he had the students complete an end-of-course survey, students indicated that they liked the journal process and that they would continue to use it for other large-scale projects later in their academic career.

Developing a Learning Culture

We had the experience but missed the meaning.

— T.S. Eliot, *The Four Quartets*

Reflection is as indispensable to great artists as it is to philosophers, diplomats, writers, and scientists. Unfortunately, it is infrequently used in schools.

— Renata and Geoffrey Caine

This book focuses on classroom life. In that sense, it is small scale. You won't learn in these pages how to restructure a whole system or school. Such policy-level reforms have been the object of great attention in recent times and probably always will be. Those who find themselves interested in large-scale topics in education will have no trouble finding sources. We want to visit with you at the level where human beings interact most closely in school life, and that is the level where teachers and students come together in the name of learning.

If your classroom were to become a place where students followed their interests within the course of study, how would it be different from the way things are now? What would happen if you allowed your students to tell you what they planned to do in order to meet the academic requirements you have established? How would you feel if your students began to tell you, consistently, that they really enjoy school?

If your classroom were to become a place of opportunity, what would that mean in a practical sense? If someone were to mention to you that your classroom is a place where choices abound and greater opportunities are found, how would you feel? If you could clearly see that your students know that your classroom is less a place of restriction than one of opportunity, would you welcome this?

If your classroom were to become a place where time is given to reflect, to think, and to analyze, how would it be different? What would happen if you decided to "cover" less ground and spend more time treating a few selected issues in depth? To what extent do you think you would be willing to turn over much of the responsibility for the assessment of academic achievement and the quality of classroom life to your students? What would happen if you did?

The first year that we taught we were always looking for art ideas that related to the academic course of study. From time to time we would go to the library and read books on various art projects in search of activities for our students, ones we thought they would enjoy and profit from. We spent hours looking for lessons that seemed particularly interesting. One that struck our fancy, and the students seemed to agree, was soap carving. You simply take a bar of Ivory Soap and go to work! Of course there is more to it than that, there are certain skills involved to be sure, and we did our best to teach those skills. And so we set about this venture. The students did some rather creative work, we thought, and we displayed their efforts on a table in the back of the room.

This was all to the good. Carving soap is therapeutic and visually expressive at the same time. But the difference between this lesson, which was reasonably good from the standpoint of active involvement and student enjoyment, and one that could have been far better was enormous. What was missing? What would we do differently now? The missing piece, the piece so often missing in the school experience, was reflection, a search for meaning. We never really reflected on the experience. We didn't take the time to talk about sculpture, and how carving as artistic expression involves reduction while painting, in contrast, involves addition. We didn't think to ask the students to talk about how they felt about their work. We didn't spend time writing or drawing about the experience. We didn't have a potter or sculptor visit the class to talk with young artists about his or her work. It didn't occur to us to show examples of sculpture by professional artists or craftsmen. In short, *we had the experience but missed the meaning*, to paraphrase the poet T.S. Eliot.

This is the essence of reflective thinking, a search for meaning. Reflection involves stepping back from what you're doing in order to achieve some measure of perspective. It means thinking, talking, and otherwise expressing your feelings, the things you've learned, the growth you've achieved, and the sense you have of accomplishing something. We are convinced that this is one of the greatest problems we face in classroom life. The problem is a failure to reflect. The remedy is to take the time to do it in spite of the fact that you and your students won't be able to "cover" as much. No amount of "fun" activities can make up for the loss that accompanies a failure to search for meaning.

This book is designed to help you with the issues of interest, opportunity, and reflection in teaching and learning. To the extent that you practice the activities found at the end of each chapter, you will begin to see positive changes in your learning environment. In all probability, you will see higher achievement by your students. Higher student achievement ought to be the goal in any educational situation. But that alone is not sufficient. We think you will also see an improved social/moral fabric in the daily life of your classroom. As students begin to act on the basis of genuine interest, as they sense the unlimited opportunities available in your classroom, and as they practice reflective self-assessment, they become more reflective in their practice, just as you do. Assessment at its best is about far more than test scores, important as they are. Assessment lies at the very heart of learning. Our hope is that you will come to think of teaching, learning, and assessment as indivisible.

Learning Community Discussion Starters

1. One argument against reflective assessment practice by students is that it takes time from covering more material. What do you think about that?

2. What kinds of adjustments would you have to make to your classroom management policy to promote student choice and decision making?

Strategy 12
Learning Illustrated

Drawings are graphic accounts of essentially verbal processes.
— Karl Buhler

Purpose

Years ago there was a comic book series known as *Classics Illustrated.* The series included the works of such notable writers as Shakespeare, Sir Walter Scott, Mark Twain, Leo Tolstoy, Jules Verne, and Mary Shelly. As a child we read most of them. We mistakenly thought, and so did our teachers, that we were well acquainted with the great books of Western literature. After all, these comic books had everything you generally needed to take part in a discussion or to pass a school exam: plot, setting, main characters, and so on. And because they were largely pictorial with a few key utterances thrown in, we even "knew" such things as how people dressed and what the architecture looked like, and had a sense of geographic setting. The few words that were spoken by the characters were usually quotable and memorable because most of the words from the real books were missing. We guess we had subscribed to the old saying, "a picture is worth a thousand words." It was the triumph of illustration over print. In time even we learned that there is more to literature than this. But it was a place to start, and it did meet a need that led to the desire in time to read the real books.

Have you ever asked a child to explain something to you and the child replies, "Well, I know but I can't explain it." The chances are pretty good that the child *does* know and could explain it although not perhaps in words. The problem for children, especially younger children, is putting what they know into words. But they do like to draw.

Let's face it, you don't have to be able to explain something orally or especially in writing to know how to do it. Many young children know how to tie their shoes, a difficult skill, but could not write a paragraph explaining how they do it. In fact, there is often little relationship between mastery of a skill and the ability to explain it. Many outstanding athletes are not particularly adept at analyzing and communicating their world-class skills. But few people would be foolish enough to say those athletes don't know what they're doing on a basketball court or skating rink.

We recall giving a map-making assignment to a class of university students. They were to go out into the environment around the university and observe, record, and map a certain portion of the landscape. When the students turned their products in to us, we were surprised that among the best maps were those turned in by students who were not necessarily anywhere near the "top" of the class. Of course, we should have known that we use biased information, heavily biased toward reading and writing skills, to determine our ideas of who the "top" students are. Intelligence and ability take many forms.

Procedure

One of the most natural modes of childhood expression is that of drawing a picture. Most children love to draw, and in most cases they have not yet formed an idea of whether they are "good" at drawing. They simply enjoy this medium of showing what they know, of expressing their thoughts and feelings. They have not acquired the verbal skills of older learners, so they depend on this method of expression. As time goes by, teachers increasingly rely on writing skills as a way of knowing what students know and feel, and decreasingly on student pictorial representation. This is unfortunate.

Anyone who has visited a good art museum can tell you that iconic expression is among the most powerful and legitimate modes of conveying an idea, mood, or sense of place. In most books, words are merely supplemented by pictures, but in an art exhibit, pictures are supplemented by a few words of explanation. In our opinion, one of the shortcomings of the Lewis and Clark journey of discovery is that President Thomas Jefferson did not make provision for a sketch artist to accompany the expedition. The journals kept by expedition members are filled with wonderful word descriptions, but just imagine the pictorial treasures we would have today: illustrations of Native Americans, the wilderness landscape of the West, the many animals and plants seen along the way, and the travelers themselves.

Without doubt, the school *assessment* tradition is heavily biased toward letters and numbers. Why wouldn't it be? School *assignments* are heavily biased toward letters and numbers. This is not meant as a complete indictment of the school experience. But far too much of the assessment protocol is weighted toward reading, writing, and numbers. Academic life always has been and probably always will be oriented primarily toward symbolic learning, but increasingly we are become more aware of the importance of other learning modes and means of expression.

Jerome Bruner (1966, 1996) argued for balance in the school curriculum among the types of teaching and learning that he calls symbolic, iconic, and enactive. His point, a familiar one, is that symbolic learning plays far too dominant a role in teaching and learning, and that even our emphasis on symbols (words, numbers) could be qualitatively improved through greater emphasis on visual and active learning. Iconic learning involves images, and enactive learning involves "hands-on" experience. It is on iconic learning, the mode represented so well in *Classics Illustrated,* that we wish to focus our attention here.

Learning Illustrated calls on students to use essentially nonverbal means to show that they have learned a concept, skill, procedure, or other content. The procedure involves sketches, drawings, maps, flow charts, diagrams, graphs, or any other iconic means of demonstrating knowledge. For example, if your students are studying weather and climate, they might select a concept such as cloud types to illustrate, making drawings of cumulus, stratus, cirrus, and other cloud formations. If students in a mathematics class are studying probability, then a task might be to make an area map of possible outcomes in a given situation, or to draw a probability tree representing the same information.

An innovative twist on *Learning Illustrated* is to ask students at the end of a lesson to draw a picture, make a flow chart, construct a diagram, create a map, or complete some other graphic rendering of the lesson. This affords them the opportunity to reconstruct the lesson in a completely novel way. It asks them to step outside the normal boundaries of thought and expression and to employ a metacognitive strategy as they reflect back on what was taught and learned.

Outcomes

There is little new in this idea. However, when such a task as illustrating something one has learned is placed within the matrix of a range of reflective strategies, then *Learning Illustrated* plays a role in providing variety and choice. Remember that the more ways you have of gaining knowledge of student learning, the better informed you will be, and therefore the better informed your constituencies (students, parents) will be. An additional outcome is that of providing a much needed nonverbal means for students to show themselves and others that they are indeed leaning.

Differentiating *Learning Illustrated*

 Having students group up and then having each student in the group contribute their individual frame to a group cartoon or series of pictures that summarizes main ideas or concepts is a great way for students to collaborate using this strategy.

Students can get creative and film a silent movie that acts out or shows off their learning in a fun and original way. Video editing software could be employed to create a short one-minute film that effectively communicates what the students want to demonstrate. Another tech option is to have students create a high-tech artistic work using one of the many available drawing or paint programs. These artworks could then be shared in a Power Point-styled art show.

 Remember that the basis for evaluation of student work is intent of demonstrating the concept and not really artistic merit. Allowing students to know that stick figures and basic drawings are accepted so long as they convey the intended meaning is critical for putting nonartistic students at ease with the assignment and how it would be evaluated.

 Asking students to produce their work in the style of a well-known artist either from their history lesson or from the literary piece you are studying adds an element of complexity to the students thought process, design, and final product.

 This strategy dovetails nicely with many of the other strategies in this book; rather than having students do writing for *I Learned* (Strategy 1) statements, *The Week in Review* (Strategy 3), or *Search for Meaning* (Strategy 9), have them illustrate or creatively depict their thoughts and ideas using *Learning Illustrated*.

From the Classroom

Margaret Combs' European history class was deep into their study of the Renaissance. The students had been energetically engaging in lively debates about humanism, secularism, and the Protestant Revolution. They had also undertaken an extensive study of the changes in art from the period, and learning about the styles of various famous painters and sculptors.

Margaret wanted to find some way for her students to incorporate their artistic learning with their learning about philosophy and religion. She developed an assessment project that would allow students to paint, draw, sculpt, or create an architectural building rendering that would be original work of the student, but reflective of a specific Renaissance artist and focused on a particular historical episode from the Renaissance.

When the projects were finished, the students had a Renaissance-themed exhibition where their parents, peers, and teachers could enjoy their work. Margaret and her students received numerous compliments from the attendees, including these comments:

I worked sooooo hard on my architecture plan, but it looks amazing! I built my own cathedral! (student comment)

The work of these students is simply stunning. I had no idea that our child and so many of her friends had such artistic talent. This is really stunning work, it really is. (parent comment)

Margaret has once again outdone herself with a clever and creative lesson, and her students delivered! I may look at stealing this idea for my classes next year... (teacher comment)

My friend Josh said that my sculpture looked like it should be in a museum. That was very cool to hear! (student comment)

I never thought that I'd be any good at an art project, because I can't draw. But when I used a ruler and worked carefully, I could make a detailed and pretty architectural plan, and that was cool. (student comment)

I continue to be impressed and amazed at the work of our students and teachers. I know that projects like this are memorable learning experiences for all involved! (principal's comment)

Margaret plans to keep this project in the repertoire for the Renaissance unit, but she hopes to make it a bit more grand in the future by incorporating a full Renaissance ball theme to the presentation night, including costuming and having students appear in character as a Renaissance personality.

Learning Community Discussion Starters

1. In your opinion, what is the relationship between academic learning and social/moral growth?

2. What are some practical steps teachers can take to make teaching, learning, and assessment a seamless whole?

Strategy 13

Clear and Unclear Windows

The eyes are not responsible when the mind does the seeing.
— Publilius Syrus ~100 BC

Purpose

Have you ever found yourself in the school hallway when a student wearing glasses comes running along and you ask her to stop for a second while you look at her glasses? Chances are they were smudged or dirty. You said something like, "Could I see your glasses for a second?" You patiently cleaned them and gave them back, asking something like, "Better?" The student says, "Yes," and runs off on her way somewhere. You say to yourself, "I don't know how she can even see where she's going." The point is that she couldn't, not very well anyway, and you made things clearer. It's a metaphor for what good teachers do all the time—*they make things clearer.*

Dirty eye glasses and dirty windows are pretty obvious to us. Our first impulse as adults is to clean them, to make them clear so that people can see out of them. We are not surprised when a student's *glasses* are not clear, even if they were clear that morning when the student left home. Why should we be surprised when their understanding of something we just taught is not clear? So much of what is taught is not clearly learned. And we think you know by now that one of the fixed ideas, one of the familiar refrains, of this book is that school is not really about teaching—it is about learning.

Procedure

The *Clear and Unclear Windows* assessment technique is simple and straightforward. At the end of an assignment or of a significant chunk of learning that may have taken place over several days, ask students to draw a vertical line on a sheet of paper and to title one half of the paper *Clear* and the other half *Unclear*. On the half titled *Clear*, a student is asked to list those things he or she understands. On the other half, the student lists those things that are not clear or are poorly understood. Students often struggle to find real-world models that inform their understanding. Ideas such as subtracting a negative and getting a larger number, or that plants receive energy from the sun and not from soil are not easily grasped. Here is where an activity like *Clear and Unclear Windows* can help. Use this strategy to informally assess student understanding at the end of a lesson, especially those that consist of particularly abstract ideas. By doing this, you will know better which ideas students understand and which need revisiting the next day. This kind of information is invaluable for helping each student understand hard-to-grasp concepts.

Nevertheless, this activity represents self-reporting. The fact that a student says he or she understands something clearly does not guarantee that the student does. However, it is a good place to start. And if someone tells you they don't understand something or that it is unclear to them, it is quite likely that they really do not understand that concept.

This particular assessment procedure assumes a great deal of trust between teacher and students. Trust lays the groundwork for effective communication and is essential to its success. No student wants to tell a teacher that something was too difficult if the result is punishment or a sense of being considered lazy or slow to learn. But wouldn't you rather know than not? Nothing is gained by pretending that everyone learned yesterday's lesson, and now we are ready to proceed to today's lesson if that is not in fact the case. When a student fails to understand a key idea or skill, especially in courses built on sequential knowledge, the student ends up paying compound interest on the learning deficit when it comes to learning the next idea or skill. Discouragement sets in and the will to learn diminishes. This is the beginning of disaster for that student's future hopes. Conversely, keep in mind that the students who indicated that they *do* understand clearly can help you with some strategic remediation to help those students who remain confused.

In the lessons you teach, everybody learned *something*. Why is it that we are so good at assessing deficits but not at rewarding learning? By giving students the opportunity to write down something they learned, you have acknowledged that they are trying. This makes them more willing to come to share what they do not know.

Outcomes

Asking students to list things that are clear to them and things that are not clear to them forces them to think about what they are learning well and where the problems lie. Self-diagnosis is a valuable skill because it enables the learner as well as those entrusted to help the learner know where to start.

Sometimes just knowing where to start is the key to unlocking deeper learning.

For example, consider this reflection by a student in a science class:

It isn't clear to me how hydrogen and oxygen go together to make water. How can two gases be put together to make a liquid? I just don't get it.

This same student had written on the *Clear* side of the sheet of paper:

I know that hydrogen and oxygen combine to make water. I know that two atoms of hydrogen are needed and one atom of oxygen, that's why it is H2O.

In many cases, learning is assumed because superficial knowledge is in place. That is exactly the situation this student is in. The student knows the words to describe water as a product of hydrogen and oxygen in combination, but the student has no clue as to how the process actually works. Maybe the teacher "covered" the process in class, or maybe not, but at least one student has indicated a lack of scientific understanding that the teacher can easily clear up in the following class period. It has been noted that even higher-achieving students in advanced science classes more often than not give medieval answers to such science questions as, "How do the seasons change?", "How does gravity work?", and "What causes night and day?" *Clear and Unclear Windows* at least gives students the opportunity to let you know about such things.

As students become more adept at writing *Clear and Unclear Windows*, they will help you take your teaching to deeper levels of knowledge and insight. This process is obviously useful with lower-achieving students who are struggling to keep up, but it is equally useful with higher achievers, many of whom will frankly confess they don't understand the subject matter very deeply and are merely good at parroting back superficial information on tests and in discussions.

Because the application of this technique, like that of others mentioned in these pages, is strategic, it is not necessary that you use it every day. In fact, one approach is to allow students to turn *Clear and Unclear Windows* statements in to you whenever they would like to. However, we do suggest that you conduct this as an activity with the class at least several times a month in order to ensure adequate opportunity for each of your students to let you know just what is clear and unclear to them.

Differentiating *Clear and Unclear Windows*

Ask students to individually create their *Clear and Unclear Windows* and pair up with one or two other students. These small groups can share out what made sense and what did not make sense to them. It may very well be that an area of clarity for one student is an area of question for another, which opens up the opportunity for peer teaching or coaching. By having the small groups discuss both clear and unclear concepts, they can then cull down the unclear elements for their group, which is likely fewer items than if all unclear items were listed from each individual. These unclear elements could then be reported to the full group for discussion.

Have students record clear and unclear concepts and then you share example statements with the class by using a document camera. This can be done anonymously to protect student feelings. But by sharing examples this way, you quickly show authentic student work to other students, which gives them an idea of where their peers are in their thought processes, as well as indicating what the you are looking for in the student work.

Teachers can make this assignment more complex by focusing on a particular topic of the lesson (e.g., characterization used in a novel or a particular cause of conflict in history) or by opening up the focus to the entirety of a unit. Allowing students to discuss their clear and unclear windows also pushes thinking toward more complex root questions that concern the "why" or causes of certain topics, which pushes the entire discussion to a deeper and more meaningful level.

Clear and Unclear Windows pairs quite well with *Think Aloud* (Strategy 2), *Pyramid Discussion* (Strategy 16), *Search for Meaning* (Strategy 9), and *Letting Questions Percolate* (Strategy 14). Combining a written document that identifies clear and unclear concepts with the opportunity to discuss those thoughts is a very powerful combination in helping students understand their thinking.

From the Classroom

Kaye Arant's students are midway through their study of the American Revolution. Throughout the unit to date, students have engaged in a variety of ways to demonstrate their learning, including writing assignments, skits, illustrations of various events or concepts, and novel study. As students moved through the unit, Kaye utilized *Clear and Unclear Windows* to help students reflect on what they did and did not know, as well as to focus on what they did and did not understand. Kaye finds that using *Clear and Unclear Windows* is simple, quick, and helps both students and herself identify areas that may need reteaching or additional time. Here are some examples from student writing:

CLEAR: I know France helped the United States win the Revolution. UNCLEAR: Why did France help us then when we don't really get along with France today? Did something happen?

CLEAR: England passed the Stamp Act and it made colonists very angry. UNCLEAR: I still don't know what the Stamp Act was. Why didn't we want stamps? We use them all of the time today.

CLEAR: Some people wanted independence and others didn't. UNCLEAR: Why didn't everyone want independence? Couldn't everyone see that Britain was greedy and treating people terribly?

CLEAR: I know the Revolution gave us independence from Britain and it began the United States as its own nation. UNCLEAR: Why did we need to have a war? Why couldn't we negotiate our freedom? What is it about territory or religion that makes compromise so impossible?

CLEAR: When there is a war, it seems like only one side wins. UNCLEAR: But how can you tell which side is right? Which side really had the truth?

Kaye took this reflective assessment further by anonymously sharing some of the student comments with the full class. She discovered that these writing samples became terrific classroom discussion starters, especially when she highlighted unclear windows that were shared by many students in the classroom. Kaye let the students collaborate and struggle on their own to discover the answers to unclear information, and in the process, she saw that students truly "owned" the knowledge by the end of the unit.

The Reflective Classroom

You can have experience without reflection, but you can't have reflection without experience.

— Maria Jacobson

Not long ago we had the occasion to visit a wonderful children's museum, one clearly dedicated to educational purposes. The place holds a wide variety of exhibits in its sizable collection, and the exhibits range from the traditional glass-enclosed showcase type to interactive, hands-on experiential learning opportunities. The museum, as you might imagine, is a popular site for field trips, and it is not at all unusual to see one big yellow bus after another lined up on the streets outside. Teachers and students alike look forward to visiting, and the museum staff are a talented, knowledgeable group perfectly able and willing to ensure that the visits are educationally worthwhile.

On the day that we there, we had some time to watch the students come and go. We were especially curious to know how they approached the task of learning in this place of exceptional sensory opportunity. Two rather different class-size groups caught our attention in particular.

The first was a class of fifth or sixth grade students; we were never sure which because there wasn't time to ask them. They literally entered the museum running, their teacher in pursuit exhorting them to "slow down a little." We quickly lost sight of the group, which seemed to be on its way to something of interest. After some time had passed, this same group came back, still at high speed, put their coats on, and left the building. One imagines they saw every exhibit possible. Obviously, they were in a hurry, but they did manage to *cover* it all, as one student breathlessly informed us as she grabbed her coat and ran for the exit.

The second group was composed of much younger children. They told us they were second graders. They and their teacher seemed to be in no hurry, and we watched them gather around several exhibit cases of ancient vases and other pottery. Each child had a sketch pad (actually a tablet) and pencil. We watched as they took it upon themselves to make careful drawings of what they viewed.

It occurred to us that this experience allowed them to take in more subtle attributes of line, shape, pattern, perspective, texture, color, size, etc. We can't say that all the drawings were suitable for framing, but that is not the point. The point is that this was a reflective experience, one in which students spent time *considering* an object worthy of examination. This group of students did not manage to see the entire museum during their visit. In other words, they did not "cover" the whole place as the older students had. But what do you really learn if you do?

So we ask you to think about the two classes visiting the museum. And as you do, ask yourself about the relative value of their very different learning experiences. All experiences teach us something, but only experiences of quality teach us something worthwhile. What are the implications for the school curriculum? Our guess is that you can answer this question on the basis of your own reflection.

Conclusion

Invariably, when people are asked to recall something interesting, useful, or lasting, in other words, something of high quality, from their own school experience, it will be an in-depth experience, perhaps a project, a concert, a play, or an athletic endeavor. And those experiences that we deem to be of high quality have another attribute: they tend to be participatory. This theme of reflection and engagement in learning runs throughout the pages of this book.

Learning Community Discussion Starters

1. Is there a sensible balance between covering content and teaching for understanding? How do you know when you have reached that balance?

2. Has the computing age changed any of the arguments regarding content coverage and content depth? Do we teach students the kinds of skills they will need in order to manage greater and greater amounts of information coming at them from multiple electronic sources?

Strategy 14

Letting Questions Percolate

My plans require time and distance.
— Walt Whitman

Purpose

Studies done years ago by Mary Budd Rowe (1987) showed conclusively that the "wait time," that is, the time between a question asked by the teacher and the first student response, is typically about 1.5 seconds. Her research showed that teachers unwittingly reward impulsivity rather than reflection. She demonstrated that when teachers extend wait time following a question to even three seconds, students give more thoughtful responses. No teacher would tell you that he or she is trying to get the students to answer as quickly as possible without really thinking about their answers. But the evidence shows that this is indeed the case.

The *Letting Questions Percolate (Percolating)* strategy helps you through the problem by giving you a concrete means of asking reflective questions that require reflective answers. Reflection takes time, and it takes consideration. Often it involves digging beneath the surface, going beyond the obvious, and making sure of one's ideas before expressing them.

Procedure

Here is how *Percolating* works. You pose a problem or question, and tell the class you *do not* want an immediate answer. You want students to take some time before answering, and you want them to do some research and reflection along the way.

For example, one approach to *Percolating* is to pose the "Question of the Week." The question of the week should be a probing question, one that seeks more than a "right" answer. The question goes up on the board or is posted in a prominent place in the room on Monday morning, and the fol-lowup discussion is held on Thursday or Friday. This gives students time to do some reading, search the Internet, discuss the matter with each other, talk to their parents, find expert opinion, and the like. It is helpful if students write down their thoughts in order to bring focus and discipline to the discussion. Questions that incorporate a moral dimension or that affect students' lives are more likely to interest them and receive due attention. Here is an example drawn from the American Association for the Advancement of Science's (1990) book, *Science for All Americans*:

> In the world of science, what are some of the problems associated with mixing fact and opinion? (This question is pertinent to many science issues, including the current debate over global climate change.)

Encourage students to look for answers in texts, in discussion with science teachers, with each other, in consultation with scientists if possible, and in finding responsible sources using Internet searches. Also encourage students to communicate their answers in as many different ways as they can. Older students "understand" immediately the importance of dividing scientific fact from opinion. However, they may not be able to give a thorough explanation or example that illustrates their thinking. Giving students time to think about the question, research an answer, and form an explanation produces a higher level of response.

A teacher posed the following question: "What could we do to get our schools more involved in our community and our community more involved in our schools?" There is an obvious difference between this question and the science question. The science question has an answer that is more definite and the "involvement" question is open to a wide variety of answers that might well differ depending upon local context. However, they are alike in that they take time to answer. This question provides students with the opportunity to interview their parents, neighbors, shop owners, and professionals in the community. This question has the potential to *create* a better sense of community.

A primary teacher posed the following question of the week: "What would it be like if you could have everything you want?" This question sent children scrambling to do some "research" in the form of talking to their parents as well as to other responsible adults and to one another. The discussion that followed later in the week was rich with examples of reflective thought on the part of young learners.

An intermediate-grade teacher posed the social studies question, "What do you think North America would be like today if the majority of the immigrants had come from Asia rather than from Europe?" The answers that came forth on discussion day included the following: (1) the idea that there would be more countries here because the high and rugged Western mountain ranges would have slowed expansion; (2) the thought that the language would probably be Chinese rather than English; (3) that "Eastern" movies would portray the Wild East; and (4) that the capital would be Las Vegas rather than Washington, DC (not sure of the basis of this thought). Because it was a hypothetical question, the kids were free to let their imaginations roam.

Outcomes

Questions or problems that require some percolating should generally relate to the context of the ideas, skills, knowledge, and values being studied by the class. By making such connections, a teacher builds in a reflective component to the course of study. Any subject worth studying has tremendous potential for probing questions and problems that require reflective thought. One test of the value of the subject matter you are teaching is its potential to raise such questions and problems.

You need to develop the questions and problems most suited to the topics you teach. However, you do not need to do it alone. This is an excellent discussion topic for a teaching team because it forces each of you to think deeper than the surface considerations. And don't overlook the creative potential of your students. They are perfectly capable of thinking up probing questions and reflective problems. We encourage you to have a box on your desk labeled *Percolating* into which students are invited to place their ideas for questions and problems.

Differentiating *Letting Questions Percolate*

You can foster a sense of "percolating" on a daily basis by having your question displayed on your interactive whiteboard or document camera and then using an online countdown timer displayed that lets students know when the question will be open for discussion in the room.

It is helpful to many students to copy down the question and/or rephrase or paraphrase the question on paper prior to discussing it. As students read the "percolating" question, they can be directed to write the question in a daily log or journal and reflect on it until discussion is set to begin. This also allows struggling learners to maintain the questions from several days, which can help them review learned information and make connections.

A variation on this strategy is for the teacher to hand out the question on slips of paper to students as they walk in the door. This sometimes catches students off guard and gets them thinking without even realizing they've been hooked!

Percolating can become part of the daily practice of a classroom. As a variation on a solid instructional practice of using wait time, teachers can routinely pose questions to the class with the caveat that there will be "one-minute of percolating" before hands can be raised or students called upon.

From the Classroom

Ruth Bugles' class is closing their study of the novel *The Sunflower* by Simon Wiesenthal. This story grapples with the large concepts of human nature, forgiveness, and interpersonal relationships in a very engaging and philosophical way. The novel is very conducive to provoking deeper questions and discussions, which made it a natural to pair with the strategy of *Letting Questions Percolate*.

Throughout the unit, Ruth posted a question every Monday using her document camera. As students entered the room, the question was displayed. Sometimes students would informally chat about the question before the bell rang, and other times students thoughtfully contemplated the question on their own. Below the question, Ruth had instructions for the students to copy the question into their learning journal. Students were then directed that the question for that day would be discussed on Thursday, and students were encouraged to bring evidence or supports for their discussion points.

The key to success, according to Ruth, is that the questions have to be open-ended and allow for divergent thinking. The questions are better when they draw on student emotion and maybe even force students to take a stand. Here are some sample questions that were discussed by the class:

Imagine that you are a concentration camp prisoner, and you come across a dying Nazi who asks for your forgiveness. What would you do? Why? (This was the first question asked prior to starting the novel.)

"In his confession there was true repentance," writes Wiesenthal. Many people think Karl was angling for "cheap grace," and that his remorse exists only because he finds himself facing death. Which point of view do you agree with? Does the very fact of Karl's expressing remorse makes him exceptional, and therefore deserving of respect?

"There are many kinds of silence," Wiesenthal states. What messages, positive and negative, does Wiesenthal's own silence convey?

What does it tell the dying man? What does it tell to you, the reader?

Ruth repeated this cycle for the three weeks of the unit, and it was so successful that she is now incorporating it into additional novel studies throughout the academic year. She disclosed that although other teachers might be afraid to provoke such deep and emotional thinking among students, she found it to be a rich learning experience that carried deep meaning for students. She found that giving students time to research, reflect, and then present their evidence in a mediated forum developed a multitude of life-long skills that translate into college and the workplace.

The Doctrine of Interest

Just as eating against one's will is injurious to health, so study without a liking for it spoils the memory, and it retains nothing it takes in.

— Leonardo Da Vinci

Da Vinci's insight brings to mind the old saying, "in one ear and out the other." If you want to stir up a group of people, especially teachers, just suggest that kids at school should be allowed to study whatever they are interested in. Suggest further that not only are they capable of deciding for themselves what they want to study, but that it is presumptuous of adults to pretend to "know" what an individual student is interested in because only the student him- or herself can know that. And finally, tell your friends that it is largely a waste of time for *any* of us to study things we are not interested in because very little true learning takes place when we do. Who knows, you may get some agreement from those to whom you tell this idea, but it is even more likely that you will start a lively discussion to say the least!

As radical as this argument seems, it is in fact a very old idea. In *The Republic*, Plato (1991) concluded that you can make people stronger by forcing them to do physical exercise, even against their will. But he warns us that you cannot force the mind; it will find ways *not* to learn. This was in the fourth century BC. Several hundred years later, the Roman orator Quintilian (1965), writing in his celebrated book, *Institutes of Oratory*, informs the reader that students should be allowed to study whatever they wish to study because anything less is a waste of both the teacher's and the student's time. He called his idea the *Doctrine of Interest*. Nothing much happened as a result of Plato's or Quintilian's advice. Teachers in the ancient world regularly force-fed the curriculum, complete with beatings and scoldings.

John Dewey, laying much of the groundwork for the constructivist paradigm, states that interest on the part of the student is "the first condition."

Dewey wrote that, "Unless the activity lays hold on the emotions and desires, unless it offers an outlet for energy that means something to the individual himself, his *mind* will turn in aversion from it, even though he externally keeps at it" (1933/1998, p. 218). Of course, Plato beat Dewey to that idea by approximately 2500 years, but it is good to learn that it has staying power.

Imagine a young person who is always drawing during class time. One way to look at that is from the point of view of off-task behavior: "Please stop drawing on everything and pay attention to the assignment." Another take, however, is: "You know, you really like to express yourself by drawing, and I think that's wonderful. We really need illustrators for our projects so I am happy that you are here." Same student, same behavior, different interpretation. Much of what happens to us in life is not the event itself but the interpretation we put on it.

Of course, students need to learn many things that they would not have chosen to learn. Adult supervision of the curriculum is necessary. But I am convinced that students are far more neutral in their likes or dislikes of school subjects than we might think. The same student who says one year that she hates science will say the next year that she loves science. She is not really talking about science, but about who is teaching it and how it is taught. When teachers establish a relational environment, students will respond accordingly.

Conclusion

The doctrine of interest seems outrageous to some people when they first hear it explained. But on deeper consideration, most of us are willing to admit that it is a powerful idea. Give students the freedom to express themselves in ways that they know intuitively represent their strengths. If we are truly concerned about *motivation* to learn and appropriate, individualized *means* of demonstrating learning, then it is up to us to provide the *opportunity.* A closing thought: Allowing students to follow their interests ought not to lead to a random curriculum. The message for the curriculum is to allow student choices within the course of study and to make learning as relational and exciting as possible.

Learning Community Discussion Starters

1. Which subject(s) do you think many kids would avoid if they were not required to take them? Why do you think that is?

2. Research shows that students are attracted to teachers who are enthusiastic about what they teach, maintain a friendly but challenging and well-ordered classroom, and who they believe care about them. How does this relate to the doctrine of interest?

Strategy 15
Record Keeping

Let's look at the record.

— Al Smith, presidential candidate

Purpose

Several years ago, one of the nation's leading medical schools reported an intriguing finding from studies of patients suffering from hypertension (high blood pressure). The obvious treatments, alone and in combination, were tried in order to determine the best courses of action for treating this dangerous illness. The treatments included medications, diet, exercise, meditation, relaxation response, and a range of other interventions, including placebos. Patients receiving treatment were routinely asked to monitor their blood pressure, taking it several times a day and recording the results on a chart.

Completely apart from their findings of the effects of the various treatments, doctors began to notice a lowering in patients' blood pressure that seemed to be associated with the record keeping itself. That is, a *correlation* was noted between keeping a record of one's blood pressure over time and a subsequent reduction in one's blood pressure. Of course, such a relationship does not imply cause and effect. How could putting numbers on a sheet of paper cause one's blood pressure to decrease? Isn't this a little like the old prediction that when soft drink sales increase so does the rate of death by drowning? The *cause* is neither; it is the warmth of the sun that causes people to drink more and swim more.

When it comes to reducing one's blood pressure, diet, exercise, and other interventions have indeed been shown to be *causative* agents. So where does record keeping come into the picture? The answer is simple: *keeping a record increases your level of awareness.* It creates a deeper level of consciousness, whereas not keeping a record often leads to an exaggerated sense of reality.

People typically underestimate the number of hours they watch television each day, but when they begin to keep a record of what and how much they watch, they typically begin watching less. Try this activity with your students. Have them estimate the number of hours they spend watching television, and then have them actually keep a record for a week. It makes for a good discussion. Good records are the beginning of good assessment.

The person who takes the time to record his or her blood pressure several times a day is far less likely to eat that doughnut, far more likely to take a walk, far less likely to kick the dog in anger, simply because he or she is more aware of the problem itself. Similarly, the student who takes the time to record time spent on homework, pages read, problems worked on, and the like, becomes more aware of the need to study. It represents a reality check, so that if we wish to improve, we have established a baseline against which to measure subsequent improvement.

Procedure

There is nothing magical about record keeping. It's just a wise procedure. It tends to reduce the gap between how one imagines one is doing and how well one is doing in fact. A report card grade ought not to be a big surprise. A student ought to know pretty much how he or she is doing in mathematics, social studies, spelling, or any other subject. Keeping the record tends to put teacher and student on the same page, so to speak. And students should be required to show their parents the records *they* keep at least once or twice during a reporting period. This way help can be given when it is really needed and not after the fact.

A very helpful activity is to have students keep records of the amount of time they spend on their homework, the number of pages they read, and so on. These kinds of records are easy enough to keep, and they do have a way of raising levels of awareness. We have tried it with students from elementary school through college and have found that when we have them keep records of time spent, pages read, and the like, they say they are more conscientious about their work.

Records are routinely kept in sports, and we should learn from the example. Everyone knows whether the team has a chance to go to the playoffs because everyone who is interested knows the team's record. Each player knows not only how the team is doing in the standings, but how he or she is doing as an individual.

We suggest that you require students to record their grades or marks on all papers, complete with topic, date, any comments, and the grade itself. As the entries reach a significant number, then they should be converted to graphs, charts, essays, or other means of showing trends. This is the raw material for discussions that students need to hold with their parents from time to time about their progress.

Of course, spelling scores, mathematics scores, and other more easily quantified items are obvious material for record keeping. A more subtle form is the idea of writing down each day a *sense* of one's progress in less quantifiable areas of the curriculum. Although this is more "subjective," it does give both student and teacher insight into the student's perceptions. As you have students do this, remind them to incorporate any kind of evidence that they can of their progress.

Outcomes

Requiring students to keep records of their achievement gives them the opportunity to work with *real* data (their own). When they compute averages, make graphs and charts, calculate where they stand in relation to a grade in a class, and write brief notes on their progress, they are *doing* the kinds of activities that we want them to learn in science, mathematics, English, social studies, and other subjects. Thus a level of transfer of learning is achieved, something that rarely happens in school life, if we can believe the critics. English philosopher Francis Bacon wrote that real inquiry always begins with facts, one's own facts. The inferences should follow the facts.

The keeping of records is also the beginning of history. In the same way that we know so much about life in ancient Egypt because the Egyptians were such careful record keepers, so, too, did the Egyptians themselves know a great deal about their lives, far more than did those other societies in which records were poorly kept. We once read of a tribe where all evidence of a person's existence, all of the person's belongings, were destroyed when the person died. The person was never mentioned again by those who knew him or her. Thus the tribe had no story because the past did not exist. There simply was no record and therefore no history.

A student who acquires and applies the record-keeping skill early on is given a method of organization that will prove useful across a range of life activities. Keeping a record of school achievement is the beginning of the student's work as a scientist or mathematician and as a person of greater awareness and deeper consciousness.

And, finally, record keeping shifts the responsibility for how one is doing to where it belongs—with the individual. This is not to say that teachers should not keep their own records; of course, they must. But it is far better to have two sets of records than one. If a student keeps good records of his or her achievement, there is little reason for surprise grades to happen. Knowing how you are doing along the way is empowering. It gives you the opportunity to make changes where and when they are needed. Socrates' admonition, "know thyself," is helped toward fulfillment when we keep good records.

Differentiating *Record Keeping*

 Students can maintain their records on whatever it is they are using to track electronically. They can do this via a wiki, a blog, or simply by entering their records into a spreadsheet. Electronic documentation allows for ease of access both at school and at home, as well as giving a stored record throughout the year. By maintaining various records, students can engage in an end-of-semester or end-of-year exercise where they examine and compare the various records they have maintained to get a clearer perspective on their learning. To facilitate this process, the teacher can provide a basic template that can be exported, copied, and pasted to get the students started.

 Students with learning disabilities really benefit from this strategy because it helps them see how and where they are spending their time. Students can quickly figure out that it might take them a very long time to complete a required reading, whereas doing questions on that reading will take very little time. This helps those students plan their individual study time more effectively. Teachers can promote this self-regulation in their students by giving them templates for tracking various data and then guiding the student in analyzing that data effectively. This will result in greater feelings of self-efficacy for these students as they then know how to plan their learning time for the greatest amount of success.

 This strategy can be as straightforward as simply tracking the number of books read, tracking the number of minutes spent on particular activities, or tracking the progress made on assessments.

 Students can keep records on any number of items. They can track numbers of pages read in a novel, they can track the amount of time they spend on various assignments, they can track the number of questions they have on a particular reading assignment or project. Students can also track their success rate on various tasks, like tracking numbers of questions they got right on a quiz or assessment or even tracking their successful attempts at finding research information on their own. Students can also track their participation in discussions in class or monitor their contributions to an online forum or discussion set up for the class (e.g., a wiki or discussion thread on a particular topic).

 This strategy can easily be combined with *Parents on Board* (Strategy 8), as parents or guardians could be responsible for confirming or signing off on student record-keeping for homework, pages read, time spent working, and so on. This enables parents to gain a clearer perspective on what their student is learning, as well as the amount of difficulty or ease that the student has with that particular unit of study.

From the Classroom

Teachers are responsible for ensuring that students learn and retain content, but teachers are also charged with helping students attain and cultivate essential academic and life skills in order to be successful in the long-term. Erica Bowser, who taught sophomore-level English, knows that her students must be able to monitor their time wisely and be able to accurately predict the amount of time it would take for them to complete certain tasks.

Early into the year, Erica began requiring a *Record Keeping* element to all homework and classwork. She asked her students to record the time it took for them to read assigned chapters or passages, as well as tracking the time it took them to complete supplemental learning activities that went along with the assigned reading. Students did this for both homework and in-class work.

Students maintain a log with four columns. Students recorded the date in the first column, the second column is where students noted the title of the reading that was to be read, the third column is where students recorded the time it took to complete just the reading, and the fourth column is where students marked the time it took for them to complete the supplemental learning activity that went along with the reading. At the close of each unit, students went back through their logs and reflected on their performance overall, noting certain trends or interesting facts about their data about themselves.

As the year progressed, Erica began to notice that students were completing their homework more regularly, and that the quality of the work was improving as well. When she talked about this fact with her students, many of them pointed to the fact that they knew how long it would take them to complete assignments, so they were better able to manage their time both in class and at home. Students also indicated to Erica that they liked the reflection on their logs as many felt they saw growth or consistency in how they did their work. This led to greater self-regulation or self-management of their time, and students told their teacher that this definitely set them up to feel like they could handle their time more successfully.

Consciousness

Consciousness is the glory of creation.
— James Broughton

One purpose of this book is to provide you with ways to raise the level of consciousness, both individual and collective, in your classroom. This is what the reflective strategies, when used faithfully, are designed to accomplish. The thesis we propose is that if you are able to create an environment in which consciousness raising is a clear theme, then you will begin to see positive results in the two areas of classroom life that are most important: *academic achievement* and *quality of life*.

The term *consciousness* is often not well understood or is misunderstood, so it seems reasonable for us to take some time to explore its meaning and implications in a learning environment. It is widely agreed that consciousness consists of three attributes: *language, self-awareness,* and *theory of mind*. All three attributes must be present and encouraged in order for a truly reflective learning environment to emerge and prosper. Let's look at each attribute of consciousness in turn.

Language

For some reason, school is one place in life where you are expected *not* to talk most of the time. In the most productive work and leisure environments, people tend to talk freely about what they are doing, thinking, or feeling, but, with rare exceptions, in school you are expected to be quiet and keep your eyes on your own work. Ironically, we know that speech develops the intellect just as the intellect develops speech. Conversation creates community; its absence creates alienation.

Self-Awareness

A second attribute of consciousness is self-awareness, that is, a fully realized sense of one's self, that *I* exist as a being separate from the world around *me*, but am at the same time connected to others and the world. Such awareness takes time to develop, and we need to be patient when it comes to children.

The work of psychologist Carl Rogers has done much to promote the idea of self-realization. In his book, *Freedom to Learn* (1969), Rogers made it clear that the primary issue in classroom life is trust. When teachers begin to trust themselves and to trust their students, a different kind of environment emerges, one in which there is far more freedom accorded the individual to initiate, choose, pursue, and reflect upon his or her learning.

Self-awareness is something that comes fairly early in life, but it must be nurtured in order to fully develop in healthy ways. The best way for a teacher to encourage its growth is to allow freedom of choice, autonomy, and self-regulation within a structured environment of trust where subjects are made appealing and where options exist by which students can meet meaningful learning goals. How can we be sure whether school learning is meaningful or not? A place to start is by asking students to reflect on such matters.

Theory of Mind

Theory of mind refers to an *awareness of others*. This is the realization that others think, have opinions, feelings, and ideas and are conscious beings.

At a deeper level lies the realization that one must take this knowledge into account in dealings with others. The implications for the classroom are enormous. Most classrooms are probably smaller than they ought to be and certainly more crowded than we would wish. The time-honored solution to this problem is to have each student occupy his or her own desk area while keeping to him- or herself. But this ignores theory of mind, ensuring that growth won't happen on any regular basis.

Cooperative learning, project learning, simulations, group inquiry, learning centers, and other team approaches that invite students to come together in the name of learning are the answer. This is why extracurricular activities are so productive and so attractive. To play on a team, to work together to produce a school newspaper, to put on a play, to be a member of a debate club, all speak to collaboration, to the opportunities to develop theory of mind, to realize that others have something to offer in life.

Conclusion

Working and playing together is a necessary but not completely sufficient condition of productive school life. Good experiences cry out for good reflection. For all three attributes of consciousness to come into play, there must be continuous emphasis on reflection, on a search for meaning, on a ferreting out of key ideas, of a sense of what one is learning and how valuable it may or may not be. This is the essence of reflective practice and the way to raise the individual and collective consciousness of students and teachers.

To take seriously the components of consciousness—that is, language, self-awareness, and theory of mind—classrooms have to be transformed. They must become places where communications skills are practiced daily, where people work together, and where they reflect on the meaning of experience.

Learning Community Discussion Starters

1. Anyone who has spent time in a classroom will agree that students are interested in talking with one another. In what ways can you take this interest and channel it so that student conversation is educationally productive?

2. Ask yourself about the ways that you build trust in your classroom. In other words, how do you encourage and promote confidence, fairness, truth, and honor?

Strategy 16
Pyramid Discussion

Discussions tend to improve when people get a chance to talk.
— Annette L. Clemens

Purpose

Class discussions provide excellent opportunities for the teacher to be both sage and facilitator. This is so because discussions usually require a careful balance between teacher direction and active student participation. A class discussion has two main purposes: (1) to exchange ideas and clarify thinking through public discourse, and (2) to maximize student participation in the exchange. Good discussions are both active and reflective.

The teacher's role in a *Pyramid Discussion* is that of skillful questioner and guide. It is a bit of an art form in reality. To ask penetrating questions, to stay on topic, and to invite as many students as possible into a discussion is not an easy task. In a room with thirty students, sheer numbers are against you. Let's say that a discussion lasts twenty minutes, which would be against the odds, but in a thirty-minute lesson this leaves about ten minutes for teacher talk and about one minute per student, assuming everyone contributes.

The problem is compounded by the reality that not every student speaks up during a typical class discussion. This occurs for different reasons, among them reluctance to speak in front of a group, uncertainty as to what one ought to say, and even the age-old inability to get one's two-cents worth in when so many people want the floor. This is why most class discussions are actually discussions between the teacher and three or four students while most of the class sits by. This doesn't necessarily mean the silent majority are not learning, but a major goal of discussion is defeated when people don't talk.

Procedure

There is a remedy for this very problem in the form of the *Pyramid Discussion*. The pyramid approach *maximizes* student talk while meeting the goal of giving *everyone* a chance to talk. Here is how it works.

The teacher (or perhaps, in time, the students themselves) prepares several key questions on the topic at hand. You do not need very many questions, perhaps two or three, but they should be strategic in that they get to the heart of the matter. The questions are placed on the board, given out on paper, or otherwise made available to every student. Each student is given a few minutes to write down his or her thoughts in answer to the questions. It is important to have students commit their ideas in writing if possible. Of course, with younger students the entire procedure is carried out orally.

After they have had an opportunity to think through their ideas alone, students are placed in discussion pairs. Dyads (groups of two) maximize each person's opportunity to speak to an "audience," however small. This discussion should take about five minutes or so as students share their ideas with a partner. This portion of the discussion is the least threatening to those students who are initially reluctant to share their thoughts with an entire class. It is easy for teachers to overlook how difficult this is for many students.

Now we begin a geometric expansion of the discussion groups. Two pairs are put together to form groups of four. After students have had an opportunity to share in a group of four, we move to groups of eight, and finally to full class size.

The teacher's role up until the group reaches full class-size is to move around the room, monitoring the groups, providing assistance when or where it is needed. Notice we skipped a group of sixteen. It isn't necessary; you can go from groups of eight to full-class discussion.

By the time we reach full class-size, every student will have had ample opportunity to think about and *talk about* the questions, thus providing several rehearsals for the discussion in which the teacher leads the entire class. This repeated practice underscores the fact that the discussion questions must be thoughtful, probing questions, ones that are worth going over several times. If we are serious about sustained, reflective thought, this process will help us meet that goal.

Outcomes

This approach to class discussion results in highly increased levels of student involvement and far more thoughtful answers to questions as well. *Everyone* participates and everyone has a chance to respond to the questions more than once. Thoughtful answers to difficult questions take time and practice. Keeping in mind Aesop's fable of *The Tortoise and the Hare,* the reward should be not to the quick but to the thoughtful. It takes time to build a reflective environment, one in which teachers and students search for meaning in depth. Using the pyramid maximizes the potential for everyone to take part in reflective discourse.

Differentiating *Pyramid Discussion*

 Teachers can use a projector and/or interactive white board to chart the pairing up of students into pairs and then into groups. Students can also record their information on the interactive white board. Students could also self-select partners or groups and then indicate who is in which group and where that group will be going in the next round on the interactive whiteboard. This process can also be done entirely online via blogs or discussion forums!

 Teachers can support struggling learners by preassigning partners and having those students participate in a pair or group that will nurture their thinking and empower them to contribute to the discussion at hand.

 This process can be simplified by preassigning the groups for students. If students know that they will be paired up with a particular peer in the ensuing class meeting, they can prepare for that discussion in advance. Conversely, teachers could have those pairs "pre-meet" via an online blog or forum, and come to class ready to meet in larger groups.

 As you read through many of the other strategies you noticed a reference to using structured discussion groups. This is, in fact, *Pyramid Discussion*! This strategy can be used in whole or in part with almost every other strategy outlined in this book. It is a fantastic way to control discussion while maximizing participation of all students in the room.

From the Classroom

James Andrews notices that students in middle school are oftentimes hesitant to chime in when there is a classwide discussion taking place. He knows that students at this particular age often are worried about how they appear to their peers, and that they will refrain from contributing to a class discussion if they do not definitively know the correct answer. After becoming frustrated following two failed attempts at engaging students in discussion, James knew he needed a different approach.

When it came time for the next discussion, James tackled it in a very different way. James posted a question for students to focus upon up on his ActivBoard, but before having students respond to the question or arrange their desks in a circle for Socratic seminar, he assigned students to a "talk partner" with whom they would discuss the question first. Students then broke into pairs. Much to James' surprise, the room was abuzz with the sound of student conversation! As he looked across the classroom, he saw all students animatedly talking, and as he listened, he heard students talking about the question that was posed.

After five minutes in their "talk partner" groups, James then had those groups pair up so that four students were now clustered together. Once again, James gave each group five minutes to continue their discussion, with an emphasis on drawing out opinions or insights from each group member. Again, the room came to life as students jumped into discussions with their peers.

Five minutes later, two groups again converged so that there were now groups of eight. To keep students focused, James gave the groups only three minutes for their conversations. At the conclusion of the eight-person groups James moved into a full class discussion. To his delight, when he asked for contributions to the discussion, he found that he had a greater number of students voluntarily contributing to the conversation. He also discovered that the quality of comments was much higher than they had been previously. "Pyramid discussion provided the pathway to participation for many of my students," says James. "I never thought that the simple act of breaking down the discussion into mini-groups would exponentially increase the number of students who would then actively participate at all levels! I am looking forward to doing this again soon." Students apparently feel the same way:

> I am a pretty quiet kid and I don't like piping up in front of groups, but talking to just one other person made it easier for me to think about and share my ideas. Pretty cool.

> Today I had a "talk partner" who I didn't know well. After we made introductions, we talked about the question that Mr. Andrews gave us. It was pretty neat to have some focused time where I could share my ideas.

> The layered discussion today was awesome! So many people talked and we heard great ideas from people who had never participated in a discussion before. Can't wait to do it again!

Conclusion

In summary, leading students in class discussion involves switching roles between sage and facilitator. Good teachers know when to adopt one role or the other, depending on the situation. Once again, balance is the key. Think carefully about what you want to accomplish with your students through class discussion. Make a plan that involves the right mixture of teacher roles to produce a positive effect on student learning using discussion.

Large class size presents a significant obstacle to class discussion. Large classes, and we have all had our share of these, can be impersonal, tough to manage, and loud. Not only that, but students get lost in the crowd of a large class. As we have mentioned, in a class of thirty kids there are usually a few students who dominate discussions while everyone else sits around. Organizing discussions around the *Pyramid* format produces more student participation.

Learning Community Discussion Starters

1. What assumptions do educational policymakers have about learning when twenty to forty students occupy one classroom? Do any of these assumptions contradict the ways that humans communicate through discussion?

2. Besides *Pyramid Discussion*, how else can teachers modify their approach to conducting classroom discussions to produce an effect?

Epilogue

There are several means by which we may gain insight and wisdom, but the first of these is by reflection, which is the most noble.

— Confucius

This is a book about practical ways to create a classroom environment in which teaching, learning, and assessment come together to form a seamless whole. It is a book about raising achievement. It is also a book about improving the social/moral fabric of classroom life. Now that you have read the book and begun to apply the strategies, you should have real insight into the potential for making this happen.

The vehicle for making these things happen is reflective practice. Reflective practice has the power to change the way you and your students act, think, and feel about school life. This is because reflective practice asks more and gives more in return than business as usual. Reflective practice means not just doing things, covering the curriculum, carrying out assignments, preparing for tests; it means digging beneath the surface to unearth questions of purpose, meaning, value, and belonging. And you don't need a grant or restructuring of the entire educational system. You merely need to give your students voice. When they feel you have invited them into the conversation and have created ways for them to become reflective, good things will occur.

It is unfortunate that even in "better" classroom situations, reflective practice is the all-too-often missing ingredient, the factor that, if it *were* present, would make the difference between school as "that place you have to go to" and school as "that place you want to go to." Reflective practice is about caring, collaboration, integration, affiliation, and truth in teaching and learning. It is about creating community where all the citizens feel empowered and needed.

When people are introduced to the strategies found in this text, they are initially of different opinions about whether they are teaching, learning, or assessment strategies. Our answer is invariably this: by integrating them you have all three at once. Reflective practice will change the way you and your students teach, the way you and your students learn, and the way you and your students assess hope, growth, and opportunity. And, finally, these are small-scale activities, with a focus on life in classrooms and how that life might be improved.

Each reflective assessment activity in its own way is designed to help you and your students step back from whatever it is that you are doing and to reflect on the experience. These are *activities;* that is, they are things you do. Some of them call for writing, others for discussion, drawing, investigating, recording, record keeping, and a variety of avenues that have potential for reflection. Each activity can be thought of as a lesson template. In other words, the activities use class time and homework in the same sense that other activities do. Some of the activities call for a higher teacher profile than others, but all of them call upon students to be active, engaged, responsible, caring learners. In yet another sense, each of the activities is designed as an assessment procedure. You will find that you and your students are asking very basic questions about *what* is being learned, *how* it is being learned, and even *why* are we learning it. We wish you and your students the best as you enter the world of reflection and experience its rewards.

Learning Community Discussion Starters

1. Which of the sixteen strategies presented in this book work for your particular teaching style? Can you begin using one of these strategies "as-is," or can you adjust it to better suit your purposes?

2. Consider your favorite instructional practices. How do these integrate characteristics of reflection and assessment already?

References and Suggested Readings

Achenbach, T., Dumenci, L., & Rescorla, L. (2004). Are America's children's problems getting worse? A 23-year comparison. *Journal of Abnormal Child Psychology, 31*(1), 1–11.

Achenbach, T., Howell, C., McConaughy, S., & Stanger, C. (1998). Six-year predictors of problems in a national sample: IV. Young adult signs of disturbance. *Journal of the American Academy of Child & Adolescent Psychiatry, 37*(7), 718–727.

Adler, M. (Ed.). (1952). Nicomachean ethics. In *Great books of the western world.* Chicago, IL: Britannica.

Ainsworth, L., & Christenson, J. (1998). *Student-generated rubrics: An assessment model to help all students succeed.* White Plains, NY: Dale Seymour Publications.

Allison, B., & Rehm, M. (2007). Effective teaching strategies for middle school learners in multicultural, multilingual classrooms. *Middle School Journal, 39*(2), 12–18.

American Association for the Advancement of Science. (1990). *Science for all Americans.* New York, NY: Oxford.

Aronson, E. (2009). *Jigsaw.* Retrieved from http://www.jigsaw.org.

Atkinson, R. K., Derry, S. J., Renkl, A., & Wortham, D. (2000). Learning from examples: Instructional principles from the worked examples research. *Review of Educational Research, 70,* 181–214.

Bandura, A. (1971). *Social learning theory.* Upper Saddle River, NJ: Prentice-Hall.

Bandura, A. (2005). The primacy of self-regulation in health promotion. *Applied Psychology, 54,* 245–254.

Beane, J. (1990). *A middle school curriculum: From rhetoric to reality.* Columbus, OH: National Middle School Association.

Beane, J. (1997). *Curriculum integration.* New York, NY: Teachers College Press.

Bond, J. B. (2003). *The effects of reflective assessment on student achievement.* Unpublished doctoral dissertation. Seattle Pacific University, Seattle, WA.

Bruner, J. (1966). *Toward a theory of instruction.* Cambridge, MA: Harvard University Press.

Bruner, J. (1996). *The process of education.* Cambridge, MA: Harvard University Press.

Budd-Rowe, M. (1987). Wait-time: slowing down may be a way of speeding up. *American Educator, 11,* 38–43, 47.

Caine, R., & Caine, G. (1994). *Making connections: Teaching and human brain.* Menlo Park, CA: Addison-Wesley.

Campbell, C., & Campbell, B. (1999). *Multiple intelligences and student achievement.* Alexandria, VA: Association for Supervision and Curriculum Development.

Campbell, L., Campbell, B., & Dickson, D. (2003). *Teaching and learning through multiple intelligences.* Boston, MA: Allyn & Bacon.

Chomsky, N. (1980). *Rules and representation.* New York, NY: Columbia University Press.

Crick, R. (2007). Learning how to learn: The dynamic assessment of learning power. *Curriculum Journal, 18*(2), 135–153.

Dewey, J. (1897). My pedagogic creed. *The school journal, 54*(3), 77–80.

Dewey, J. (1933/1998) *How we think* (Rev. ed.). Boston, MA: Houghton Mifflin.

Dewey, J. (1938, 1997). *Experience and education.* New York, NY: Touchstone.

Dewey, J. (2004). *Democracy and education.* New York, NY: Dover. (Original work published 1915.)

Doing What Works Clearinghouse. Articles retrieved from http://dww.ed.gov.

Drucker, P. (1990). *The new realities.* New York, NY: Perennial Library.

Ellis, A. (1991). Evaluation as problem solving. *Curriculum in Context, 19*(2), 30–31.

Ellis, A. K. (2010). *Teaching and learning elementary social studies* (9th ed.). Boston, MA: Pearson Education.

Evans, L. (2009). *Reflective assessment and student achievement in high school English.* Unpublished doctoral dissertation, Seattle Pacific University, Seattle, WA.

Flavell, J. (1976). Metacognitive aspects of problem solving. In L. Resnick (Ed.), *The nature of intelligence.* Hillsdale, NJ: Erlbaum.

Gardner, H. (1991). *The unschooled mind: How children think and how schools should teach.* New York, NY: Basic Books.

Gardner, H. (1999). *Intelligence reframed: Multiple intelligences for the 21st century.* New York, NY: Basic Books.

Gardner, H. (2006). *Multiple intelligences: New horizons.* New York, NY: Basic Books.

Glasser, W. (1969). *Schools without failure.* New York, NY: Harper & Row.

Glasser, W. (1986). *Control theory in the classroom.* New York, NY: Harper & Row.

Goleman, D. (1998). *Working with emotional intelligence.* London, UK: Bloomsbury.

Goodlad, J. I. (2004). *A place called school.* New York, NY: McGraw-Hill.

Green, S. K., & Gredler, M. E. (2002). A review and analysis of constructivism for school-based practice. *School Psychology Review, 31,* 53–70.

Gregory, A., & Ripski, M. (2008). Adolescent trust in teachers: Implications for behavior in the high school classroom. *School Psychology Review, 37*(3), 337–353.

Harp, B. (Ed.). (1994). *Assessment and evaluation for student-centered learning* (2nd ed.). Norwood, MA: Christopher-Gordon Publishers.

Hoerr, T. (1994). How the new city school applies the multiple intelligences. *Educational Leadership, 52*(3), 29–33.

Johnson, D., & Johnson F. (1999). *Joining together: Group skills.* Boston, MA: Allyn & Bacon.

Langer, E. (1998). *The power of mindful learning.* Cambridge, MA: Perseus Press.

Marzano, R. J., Pickering, D. J., & Pollock, J. E. (2001). *Classroom instruction that works.* Alexandria, VA: Association for Supervision and Curriculum Development.

Maslow, A. (1973). Theory of human motivation. In R. J. Lowery (Ed.), *Dominance, self-esteem, self-actualization: Germinal papers of A. H. Maslow.* Monterey, CA: Brooks/Cole.

Maslow, A. (1987). *Motivation and personality* (3rd ed.). New York, NY: Harper & Row.

Mayer, R. (2003). *Learning and instruction..* Upper Saddle River, NJ: Pearson Education.

McClelland, D. (1973). Testing for competence rather than for intelligence. *American Psychologist.*

Pellegrino, J. (2006). *Rethinking and redesigning curriculum, instruction, and assessment: What contemporary research and theory suggests.* Paper commissioned by the National Center for Education and the Economy. Retrieved from http://www.skillscommission.org/study.htm

Phillips, D. C. (Ed.). (2000). *Constructivism in education.* Chicago, IL: University of Chicago Press.

Piaget, J., & Inhelder, B. (1968). *The psychology of the child.* New York, NY: Basic Books.

Piaget, J. (1965). *The moral judgment of the child.* New York, NY: The Free Press.

Plato (1991). *The republic.* Chicago, IL: Encyclopaedia Britannica.

Porter, A. (1993). *Reform up close: An analysis of high school science and mathematics classrooms.* Madison, WI: Consortium for Policy Research in Education.

Porter, A., & Smithson, J. (2001). *Defining, developing, and using curriculum indicators.* Madison, WI: Consortium for Policy Research in Education.

Prochaska, J. et al. (1994). *Changing for good.* New York, NY: Avon.

Quintilian. (1965). On the early education of the citizen-orator: Institutio oratoria (J. Murphy, Ed., J. S. Watson, Trans.). Indianapolis, IN: Bobbs-Merrill.

Rogers, C. (1969). *Freedom to learn.* Columbus, OH: Merrill. (See also later editions of this classic work, published in the 1983 and 1994.)

Rousseau, J. J. (2004). *Émile* (B. Foxely, Trans.). London, UK: Everyman.

Schumacher, E. (1973). *Small is beautiful.* London, UK: Blond and Briggs.

Schumacher, E. F. (1989). *Small is beautiful: Economics as if people really mattered.* New York, NY: Harper Collins.

Simon, S., Howe, L., & Kirschenbaum, H. (1972). *Values clarification.* New York, NY: Hart Publishing.

Spady, R., Kirby, R., & Bell, C. (2002). *The search for enlightened leadership.* Seattle, WA: The Forum Foundation.

Stevenson, H. (1994). *The learning gap: Why our schools are failing and what we can learn from Japanese and Chinese children.* New York, NY: Touchstone Books.

The Harris Education Research Council: Survey of American Employers. (1991). *An assessment of American education.* New York, NY: Author.

Thut, I. (1957). *The story of education.* New York, NY: McGraw-Hill.

Tindal, G., & Nolet, V. (1996). Serving students in middle school content classes: A heuristic study of critical variables linking instruction and assessment. *Journal of Special Education, 29*(4), 414–432.

Tynjala, P. (2008). Perspectives into learning at the workplace. *Educational Research Review, 3*(2), 130–154.

Whitehead, A. N. (1929). *The aims of education.* New York, NY: Mentor Book.